They Stole
My Innocence

They Stole My Innocence

The shocking true story of a young girl
abused in care

MADELEINE VIBERT

WITH **TONI MAGUIRE**

EBURY
PRESS

1 3 5 7 9 10 8 6 4 2

Ebury Press, an imprint of Ebury Publishing
20 Vauxhall Bridge Road
London SW1V 2SA

Ebury Press is part of the Penguin Random House group of companies
whose addresses can be found at global.penguinrandomhouse.com

Penguin
Random House
UK

Copyright © Madeleine Vibert and Toni Maguire 2016

Madeleine Vibert and Toni Maguire have asserted their right to be
identified as the authors of this Work in accordance with the Copyright,
Designs and Patents Act 1988

First published in French by City Editions in 2015

This edition published by Ebury Press in 2016

www.eburypublishing.co.uk

A CIP catalogue record for this book is available from the British Library

ISBN 9781785033513

Typeset in India by Thomson Digital Pvt Ltd, Noida, Delhi

Printed and bound in Great Britain by Clays Ltd, St Ives PLC

INTRODUCTION

There are reasons why my memories are jumbled, why when I try to put them in order it is the bad ones that come to me first. So, in what follows, a date may not be correct or the sequence of events may be the wrong way round. But everything happened as I say it did.

My name is Madeleine. This is my story. A story I believed would never be told. For years I buried it deep, for it is not mine alone. There are others, who were part of the horrors that haunt me still, left on the island. But, by unspoken consent, we had all agreed that the truth of what happened was never to be revealed.

Some, in their desire to eradicate their memories, have lost themselves. Alcohol, tranquillisers or whatever it took to see the past through a misty haze. And finally, when nothing proved enough, suicide has not been unknown. Of course, a lucky few have shut the door on that dark room where their memories are stored and left – but I am not one of them.

For years, half a lifetime, I believed I was safe, that what was buried would remain so. Then the police found us. One by one we were questioned. They asked for names and dates. They wanted the truth, they said.

I could start my story when I was three months old and taken into care. I could begin with my earliest memories of those happy times in my childhood when there were two women I called Mummy, or when I was five and went to live in the huge, bleak, grey building named Haut de la Garenne. Maybe it should start on the day Colin Tilbrook sent for me and fear entered my life, or when I first met the men who saw Haut de la Garenne as their private playground.

But my story really began before I was born, when a young woman left Ireland to seek a better life and, in another small Irish town, a man bade farewell to his family and travelled to Jersey.

My mother told me, years later, that she was listening to the new Doris Day song, 'Que Sera Sera' that day. Swaying to the music, she carefully placed her few clothes in a battered brown case, as she dreamt of the rosy future she was convinced would be her destiny. She smiled as she listened to the words of the hit record. Without having to ask her mother, she already knew that, with her generous curves, shoulder-length hair, black as a raven's wing, and those thickly fringed blue eyes, she was more than just pretty. But, like the song, she also wanted to know whether she would, one day, be rich. Would she live in a big house and dress like the women she had seen in glossy magazines? Not if she remained in Ireland, she thought. It was Jersey she was going to, where she had been told that a young Irish girl's dreams could come true.

Of course she would miss her family. The day before, her aunts, uncles and cousins had squeezed themselves into the house to say their goodbyes. Her mother had cooked her favourite meal – a huge rabbit stew that had fed everyone. Its mouth-watering aroma, mixed with the tang of last night's peat fire, still lingered in the room. It was nights like that she would miss most. But if she wanted a bright future, then leave she must.

She was only too aware of what the future would hold, should she stay. She had known too many pretty girls who, seeing no deeper than the charm that made them feel special, ignored their mother's advice and married good-looking rogues. Within a year they, like their mothers before them, had turned into pale-faced drudges who, except for attending church or fetching the groceries, barely left the house.

No more dancing in the white marquees, erected in local farmers' fields, on a Saturday night. Once a ring was on her finger, a woman's life consisted of producing a squalling baby each year, washing stinking nappies from the never-empty bucket and working from dawn to dusk, cooking and cleaning. Then she no longer felt special. She was just a housewife with chapped hands, lank hair and a thickening waist.

Marriage agreed with those men who wiled away time and the housekeeping money in Seamus's bar. There, while their wives spent their evenings patching and darning, the men downed the pints of Guinness called, by my grandmother, 'the curse of Ireland'. My mother could see why they were contented. No one told them what to do – for weren't they the masters of their homes? Meals were always ready for them, their clothes washed and ironed, and their children never dared answer them back. Nothing more than men's slaves: that was how my mother saw those women.

It was not a life she wished for herself and, once away from her parents, who knew what might happen? Look at Marilyn Monroe. She had come from nothing, and hadn't my mother been told by more than one boy that she was just as sexy as Marilyn, even though it was Elizabeth Taylor she resembled? Or so Patrick O'Malley had told her when he had taken her to see *I Remember Paris* at the Globe.

No, she was going to the right place, a sunny island where there was plenty of work and people lived in nice houses with indoor bathrooms. Not like her parents' small stone house, with its outside lavatory and tin bath.

How she hated the weekly ritual of the family bathtime, when she helped her mother to lift pan after steaming pan to fill the tub. Never again would she have to immerse herself in water made grimy by several bodies before her. Soon she would have a hot bath every day, be able to buy nice clothes, and when eventually she did marry, it would be to a man of means, who would look after her every desire.

Oh, yes, my mother was happy that day. I think it was the last time she was.

When she left, her mother stood in the doorway, kissed her goodbye and, like all Irish mothers whose daughters were leaving the nest, told her to write every week, to be good, and 'not to be going with any boys'.

Her father carried her case to the bus stop. As the single decker came into view he said gruffly that she was to remember she always had a home there, should she ever want to come back. Then, with a lump in her throat, she was on the bus, staring out of the window as the village where she had been born grew smaller and smaller.

It was the time of year when the winter months' endless rain had cleared, leaving lush green hedgerows, the leaves gilded by sunlight, almost hiding the clumps of wild flowers that had pushed small yellow and pink faces through the soil. As the bus trundled along the windy

CHAPTER ONE

It was a warm summer morning when my mother, with seven other women, arrived in Jersey. The sky was a milky blue. The sun, already high in the sky, shone on the rocky islet where the grey stone castle stands and turned the sparkling sea into a carpet of diamonds. The queasiness she had felt on the journey left her, to be replaced by a shivery excitement. Everything was too bright, too vivid to be real, but oh-so-beautiful.

One of the women grabbed her arm. 'Look, Maureen, look over there! Can you not see it? It's France!' One by one the rest of the women turned, shielded their eyes with their hands and, as they squinted against the sun's brightness, their murmurs of excitement rose in the air.

'Why, we could go to Paris on our day off!' said my mother, not knowing that Paris was a very long way from the Normandy coastline.

Then, with a final bump, the ship was moored and the ramp lowered. Carrying their cases, the women walked down it and, for the first time, stepped onto Jersey soil.

Looking around, they searched for the people they had been told would meet them. They knew that their lodgings had been arranged for them and all they wanted was to be taken there. Once they arrived they could have hot baths and then, they had agreed, meet up and explore the town.

Not only did they feel that this was a new beginning but, for the first time in their lives, they were free, for Ireland was strict with its daughters. No hard liquor and only a loose woman would venture into that male domain, the pub. Even the dances the girls were allowed to go to served only soft drinks. On those nights, one or both parents would be waiting up to ensure that their daughter had come straight home and that her breath was untainted by the men's smuggled-in alcohol. Now they were free of those restrictions. No curfew, no parents watching the clock. It was, my mother had told me, an exhilarating feeling.

As the chattering group waited, they saw two men walking towards them. One, somewhere in his thirties, was of stocky build, with a flushed, weather-beaten face and greasy dark hair. My mother hardly gave him a glance – she kept that for the second: taller than his friend by several inches, with the floppy light brown hair that gives even a thirty-year-old a boyish look, and a wide white smile. If Nature had been kind in giving him regular features, a cleft chin and warm brown eyes, the sun had been equally so. Instead of the ruddy skin of his friend, it had turned the visible parts of him – face, neck and forearms – a dark golden brown. He was, my mother told me many years later, simply the most handsome man she had ever seen.

'You'll be the ones from Ireland, then?' he asked, and at their enthusiastic nods, the white smile flashed again. 'Call me Jim,' he said and, jerking his finger towards his more taciturn friend, he introduced him as Bob. Neither of the two men asked the women for their names.

'Well, girls, it's our job to take you to where you're staying. I expect you're all in a hurry to get there, so just follow us.' And, with long strides, he led them to an open truck with a couple of wooden benches running along each side.

'In you hop,' he told them, then climbed in beside the older man who, still without speaking, started the engine. The last stage of their journey had started.

I only have my mother's memories as to how Jersey looked then, but I can picture that day almost as clearly as if I had been there. The harbour, very much a working one then, was very different from how it is now. I know it today, with its sleek yachts where, in the daytime, men in clean white jeans and T-shirts busy themselves coiling rope and greasing thick chains. The town of St Helier, too, must be very different, with its pavement cafés, brightly lit restaurants, designer boutiques and imposing hotels, from what it was when my mother arrived.

Behind my eyes, I can see the blue of the sea reflected in the sky and the group of girls, wearing now rather creased clothes, hair blowing in the summer-scented breeze, faces alight with anticipation for what lay ahead. In the middle of them stands my mother who, with her gurgling laugh and sparkling eyes, was the brightest of them all.

I can imagine those girls, for they were little more than that, throwing their cases into the truck, then giggling and joking as they clambered in. On the drive, inhaling diesel fumes and salt sea air, they would have seen, instead of the large pale houses with manicured lawns, tennis courts and swimming-pools that stand there now, green fields with fawn cows grazing on one side and long stretches of golden beaches on the other.

The truck reached country lanes, and at the end of one, a large farmhouse came into view.

'Nearly there,' said the driver.

'Nearly where?' Marie muttered. 'Sure, we can't all be working in that house.' She turned to my mother. 'What did they tell you, Maureen? The people who got you the job?'

'That I would start off working in the farmhouse and then, after a while, once my fare is paid back, I would be free to look for other work. As soon as I had a bit saved up for my own place, that is.'

The driver, overhearing them, laughed. 'My God, the stories they tell you girls,' he said, over his shoulder.

My mother chose to ignore him, for she was more concerned with where they were. 'We wanted to look round the town once we're settled,' she said. 'How far is it?'

'There's no distance too far to walk in Jersey,' Jim said. 'Why, the whole length of the island is only a few miles.'

'And,' his friend added. 'Are you not all used to walking in Ireland? Anyhow, first you have to see your new homes, don't you?'

There was something in the men's voices that made my mother feel uneasy. They had started talking to each other in a language she didn't understand, but she sensed by the bursts of laughter and the glances over their shoulders that it was the women who were the source of their merriment. The others also seemed to suspect that they were being mocked and fell silent.

Their uneasiness lifted when, with that smile, Jim turned and winked. 'Now don't start looking down, girls. Not on your first day here. We're only teasing you. If you all cheer up, come the weekend, I might just be talked into giving you all a lift into town. I could show you St Helier's sights.'

A chorus of thanks greeted him, and a few minutes later the truck pulled up in front of a row of oblong huts. 'Here you are, ladies, your new homes,' said Bob, unsmiling, as he climbed out of the truck.

My mother caught a sardonic gleam in his eyes when he noticed their expressions.

With walls made of concrete and corrugated-iron roofs, they did not resemble any home my mother had seen. They were more like the outhouses where, in Ireland, the deep-litter chickens were kept.

'Ach, they're not so bad, girls,' said Jim, seeing their dismay. 'Come on, have a look inside. You'll see they can be made right cosy. There's food been got in for you, so you can make yourselves something to eat and rest a bit. Remember, you have to be up early.'

'How early?' asked Marie.

'Six thirty sharp.' Before he could hear the groans, Jim swung himself back into the truck and, with a roar, it was off.

Inside, contrary to Jim's reassurance, it was little better. The door opened straight into a gloomy room, painted what my mother called a 'dull, dirty beige'. It was furnished sparsely with a dark wood table, four chairs and a sagging two-seater settee. Under the only window, which was hung with thin floral curtains, there was a cooker and sink. Two bedrooms led off it, so small that there was little space between the narrow single beds.

The first of my mother's dreams vanished, that of having her own room, as did the second, the one of luxuriating in a deep bath, when she saw what was under the ledge by the sink: a tin tub.

The next morning they found out what they had left the poverty of Ireland for. They were all to work on the farm, not in the house. Depending on the season, they were either to plant potatoes, pick potatoes, scrub potatoes or pack potatoes. When winter came, bringing with it frozen pipes and frost that crackled beneath their feet, they dressed in as many clothes as they could find to work in unheated barns. Their cold-stiffened fingers packed potatoes into wooden boxes ready for planting when spring arrived.

'Why,' my mother had said, when she'd told me how it was then, 'we'd left Ireland to get away from that. We were so gullible, believing we would be getting jobs in fancy shops and learning office work. But it wasn't all our fault – we had been asked what skills we had and most of us had some. But, no, every one of us who came across that day was put to work from dawn to dusk tending their so-called 'superior' spuds.

'The only thing we had to look forward to was going into town on payday. And that, Madeleine, was when we found out just what the locals thought of us. Scum, that's what we were, dirty Irish scum. They pointed at us in the street, you know, all of us immigrant workers who dirtied our hands doing work they were too stuck up to do.' Her eyes held a far-away dreamy look, as they always did when she talked about those early days.

'So, she continued, 'if they didn't want to mix with us, we didn't want to mix with them. We made a part of St Helier ours by turning small pubs into Irish ones. The French took over another area – it was called French Lane. It was to those places that the farm workers went on payday. Not just Irish, but the French and, later, the Portuguese as well. A right babble of different tongues, it was, in there. The locals gave those places a wide berth, I can tell you. Us girls thought we were so sophisticated, sitting in the bars with our shandy in one hand and a French Gauloise in the other.'

'Was that where you had your first drink?' I asked.

'Yes, darlin', it was,' she replied. 'The first, but not the last, more's the pity.'

CHAPTER TWO

2008

The first time the police invited me to help with their enquiries, I was not asked to come to the Jersey police station, but to some premises they used at Broadcasting House. They said that, for an informal meeting such as ours, 'It'll be more relaxing.'

On my arrival I was led into what seemed, with its couch, armchairs and coffee-table, a small, cosy sitting room. That was until I saw the tape recorder.

Two people were going to interview me, a man and a woman, who sat in the armchairs while I took my place on the settee. I remember it being uncomfortable, lower than the chairs, with a sloping seat that made it difficult to sit upright. Thick mugs of tea appeared and, wanting to delay the questions as long as possible, I stirred in the sugar slowly, then sipped it.

With some relief I noticed an ashtray on the table and, without asking, lit up. I sucked hard at my cigarette, letting its acrid tang soothe my frayed nerves, blew out a cloud of smoke and steeled myself for the first question.

I heard the click of the tape recorder being switched on, then I was asked by the woman police officer, whether I was ready. I glanced towards her, but not able to meet her eyes, lowered my gaze. A hot flush of embarrassment suffused my face as I saw what my nervousness had made me miss; the non-smoking sign.

"Oh God," I said, my fingers trembling as I ground the cigarette out on the top of my packet. "I'm sorry, so very sorry, I didn't notice," and with every stuttered word, my little spurt of nicotine-induced confidence evaporated. She made no comment to ease my discomfort. She simply asked again if I was ready.

They wanted to know about Colin Tilbrook and those rich businessmen who had visited the home, I thought.

The silence, while I waited for the first question, was loud in my ears. I could hear my heart beating, feel the moisture on my hands, and suddenly the room was unbearably hot. I wished I had asked for water. I would have been able to press a cold glass to my cheek, which felt aflame.

The first question came – not from the woman, as I had expected, but from the man.

'Tell us about the Jordans, Madeleine,' he said.

The Jordans had arrived at the home during Tilbrook's reign. That name conjured up the sound of screams, the half-lives of damaged children, broken bones no bigger than a bird's, and the helpless sobbing of those who knew nobody cared.

But I still didn't understand, at least not then, why it was them they were asking about. The Jordans had arrived in my life much later than the people I'd thought they wanted to expose. And, bad as they were, surely they were not the most important of those who had inflicted so much pain and suffering.

'We want to see if there's enough evidence against them to bring them in for questioning,' the woman said. Perhaps she'd seen my confusion on my face.

'What – just them?' I asked, in disbelief. But I didn't need to wait for the answer. I felt a burning anger in my stomach. It was not those two I had come to be questioned about. If we had been listened to, if any action had been taken, I would never have met them. I'd said as much before I could stop myself.

'Madeleine, you were placed in the crèche for your own safety.'

This time it was the woman speaking. In my head, I heard the words, 'Your mother was an unfit one; a woman who loved the bottle more than you.' And, believing that was what she was thinking, I glared at her.

That was when I realised that neither she nor the man in his dark blue suit and sparkling white shirt would be satisfied until they had cracked open the shell that, over the years, I had managed to build and dug out every last one of my secrets. Then they, not I, would decide what to do with them.

The man's voice broke into my thoughts. 'You were placed back with your mother more than once, weren't you Madeleine? But it just did not work out.'

And I knew what he meant was that my parents were criminals because they had done time.

'No,' I said emphatically. 'My mother was not a criminal.'

'So what was she, then?'

'She was sad,' I replied.

My childhood mother might still have harboured the fantasy of meeting a man rich enough to look after her, but the older one was only too aware that a blend of naïvety and avarice had led her to catch Tragedy's wandering eye. Only alcohol, which she convinced herself was a temporary measure, allowed her to dream once more of a rosy future, until her 'best friend' became her worst enemy and mocked her for her dependence.

I had asked her, with some degree of self-interest, why she had never returned to Ireland. If she had, how different my life would have been. The other question I wanted answered was why, when she had escaped a world she saw as narrow, she had married the first man she had met. Surely there must have been more to it than that he was simply the best-looking fellow she had ever seen.

It was Jim with whom she walked into the register office just three months after arriving in Jersey. 'He was a local lad,' she had said, in a voice grown deep and raspy, 'not Irish. I didn't want one of them, you see. If you go out with an Irish man, you end up talking to other women while they play darts or snooker with their friends. Now Jim, he knew how to treat a lady. And that's what he called me, a lady!' When his name was mentioned, her eyes would take on that faraway misty look and her mouth lifted in a smile, as she delved through the layers of her memories to when she was nineteen.

'I was too good to work in the fields, he told me,' she said proudly. 'And I still wanted to better myself. Oh, Madeleine, you should have seen him the way he was then, opening doors for me, bringing flowers – why, he said that the first moment he clapped eyes on me he was simply besotted. Yes, he promised me the earth, all right. Said he was going places, that his boss thought the world of him. And once I was his wife, no one would dare call me "Irish scum" again.'

'And you believed everything he told you?'

'Yes, I did. Maybe I should have asked why a register office, but he was not a Catholic, I was young and he was so very handsome.'

So my mother had done what she had left Ireland to escape from: she had seen no deeper than the charm of a good-looking rogue, who made her feel special.

Her parents were not there for the wedding, and neither were his. That should have told her something, but any misgivings were pushed firmly aside.

Less than a year after the marriage she was washing nappies, cooking and cleaning from dusk to dawn. The romance faded and, with each of her two pregnancies, grew even fainter. My mother no longer went dancing down French Lane on a Saturday night. Instead she darned and sewed, while her husband spent his money on beer and whisky.

Less than five years after she had said, 'I do,' the man who had promised her the earth left the island in search of pastures new. Pastures where there was clearly no room for a wife and two sons.

Without him, she was, once again, just an Irish immigrant.

There were no relatives, no one to lend her money for food or rent and, most importantly, no one to give her moral support. Her mother, aunts, cousins and siblings were in Ireland and, however homesick she might have been, however lonely, however desperate, she could not return there. In the late fifties her register office marriage was not recognised in Ireland by the Catholic Church. As far as the Church was concerned, she had been living in sin and borne two bastards. No amount of Hail Marys would gain her forgiveness for that in the village she came from.

So my mother had few choices. She had to remain in Jersey and, if she wanted to eat, she had to return to work. Her two children, with the help of their paternal grandparents, were placed in care. As the sons of a Jersey man, they were not sent to Haut de la Garenne, which was for problem children and the sons and daughters of immigrant families. That was the one thing their father given them: his name.

CHAPTER FOUR

My mother returned to the back-breaking work at the farm. The only way out was, she knew, to find another husband. She was also aware that a Jersey man was out of the question. She needed to find someone who had just arrived from Ireland. Someone who knew little about her history.

After a spring of planting Jersey royals, my mother knew she looked good. Hard work had toned her body and the sun had put a glow into her cheeks. Unlike the other girls who worked alongside her, she had not allowed her face to become weather-beaten or her hands to be ingrained with soil. She scrubbed her grimy nails with soap and lemon juice, and smothered every part of her that the sun touched with liberal amounts of Pond's cold cream.

She looked as good as new, she decided, when she took herself to a dance at the Irish centre. On the night that she described to me, she was wearing a red and blue tartan dress, with a low, square neckline and, over layers of stiff petticoats, a wide, swirling skirt. Laughing, she had drawn another girl up to dance. 'After all, Madeleine,' she had told me, 'sitting demurely on a wooden chair, waiting to be asked, was never going to get me noticed!'

It worked. When a hand tapped on her shoulder, she turned and looked into the green eyes of the man who became my father. Under the silvery light of the sparkling glitter ball, she smiled, pouted and swung her hips to the beat. Then the lights dimmed as the band changed to a slow number: Paul Anka's latest song. She smiled at the green-eyed man, rested her head on his shoulder and nestled closer.

When she was granted a divorce, the green-eyed man proposed and she happily accepted. Her priest, knowing my mother's wishes, sought permission for her to be married in church. His request was granted: the Catholic Church hadn't recognised her first marriage as it had taken place in a register office. Her new husband, like Jim, promised her a future; vowing that he was not going to be a labourer for ever and that, one day, he would provide her with a decent home. All they had to do was save a little.

They started married life in what was called a 'flatlet'. It was up two flights of stairs in a building permeated with the smell of boiled cabbage and fried onions from the kitchens of the Irish immigrants. Later, when the Portuguese came, roasting garlic, olive oil and espresso coffee scented her home. Grubby, cracked lino covered the floor of the entrance hall, while the pattern on the worn stair carpet was undetectable. On one side of the first landing was the shared phone, with scribbled numbers decorating the walls, on the other the communal bathroom, with its shilling-devouring meter.

On the next landing a door led into their flat. An oblong room, with scratched wooden furniture and a sagging settee. Behind a curtain there was a double bed, and under the window, a Baby Belling cooker and a sink.

It did not take my mother long to realise that, once again, she had married a wastrel. One who expected a meal on the table and no questions asked as to his whereabouts when he staggered home long after dark. That, she decided, was not the life for her and she refused to give up either work or her pay packet. Come payday the bars called to him, and this time my mother was not going to be left in that small, cheerless flat. The nicely brought-up young girl, who never touched hard liquor, had been left in Ireland, along with her dreams. She, like her husband, went to the places where drinks were cheap and the company raucous.

It was on one of those drunken nights that I was conceived. I believe my mother loved me the moment I was placed in her arms, for that is what she told me. Sadly, though, the strain of caring for a baby in a home that was almost too small for a couple, and the constant shortage of money, proved too much for my parents. They drank, they fought, they screamed and cursed until a neighbour, fearing for the safety of the three-month-old baby, called the police. Confronted by two drunken adults and the wailing child, lying in a makeshift cot, they arrested my parents and charged them with drunk and disorderly behaviour.

One month inside was the magistrate's sentence, with scant thought to my welfare. I was taken into care.

On her release, my mother begged for my return. 'Not until you have a proper home,' said the state, without telling her how, on their low income, she and my father could achieve that. Social housing was given only to those who had been resident for ten years and flats were out of my parents' price range. So I remained in care at the Westaway Crèche.

CHAPTER FIVE

2008

'Well, Madeleine, if the state didn't see your mother as a criminal, it certainly saw her as an unfit mother. Every one of her children was taken away. Now, you seem to think it was somehow the fault of the welfare system, that what happened to you was caused by the state. But let us just recap on what really happened.

'You went to Westaway Crèche when you were just three months old. Do you know why that was, Madeleine? It was not because Jim had left her, was it? After all, he was not your father. That might have been the reason her sons were taken from her, but not you. She had married again and your parents were still together when you were born.'

It was the policewoman who was talking, and although she was only calmly reciting facts, to me her words felt like barbed weapons. And each one found its mark and hurt. Tears prickled behind my closed eyelids. I swallowed them, determined that those people were not going to see me cry.

'But why did you put me in Haut de la Garenne?' I wanted to ask. I hadn't done anything wrong. I was only five.

'Now, Madeleine, I believe you were well looked after in Westaway, were you not?'

She was right. The memories of my early years might be indistinct, buried under the layers of what came later, but her questions brought images of that time back into my mind. The young nursery nurses who came and went and were kind to us, read stories out of large picture books, played games, built sandcastles on the beach, hung daisy chains around our necks, bandaged cut knees, wiped tears, blew small noses and tucked us up in bed before bestowing goodnight kisses on rosy cheeks.

The one constant in our lives was Mrs Peacock, or Mummy Peacock, as I called her. She was the one who was strict. She was also the one who let us play with her dogs and looked away when we were given a sweet too many by a younger member of staff. There was never any shortage of toys either: many were donated to the home, as were clothes and books. With thirty children in the crèche there was a birthday party nearly every week. Jellies, cakes and ice cream were set out, and tiny children were asked to blow out candles, though there were never more than five.

Apart from Christmas, when generous local residents arrived with individual parcels, all toys had to be shared and at the end of each day were deposited in the large toy box that sat in a corner of the playroom. Small children, who had yet to learn the concept of sharing, snatched and pushed and cried when told to wait their turn.

Even worse were the howls of protest when they wanted to ride on the rocking horse that a smiling benefactor had brought. I had loved it, and smiled now as I remembered my small self, screaming when told to give another child her turn. A nursery nurse had firmly lifted me off. I think that, by the end of the horse's first day at the crèche, she was finding it more than taxing to try to instill some degree of generosity into tiny pre-school children. Certainly that horse was responsible for a lot of tears and quarrels.

'No,' I said, uttering the words they wanted to hear. 'We never wanted for anything. I was happy there.'

There had been one thing I had wished for, though, but it was not something I would share with the police. I had wanted a home, one with a mother and a father, where I would have a room of my own, where my own rocking horse waited for me to ride it, and I had toys I wouldn't have to share. I knew other children went to such places. That was when they were adopted. I knew what that word meant. All of the children of about my age did. It was when a well-dressed couple came, looked at us, gave us sweets and picked up small children to cuddle. A few weeks later, a child, if old enough to understand, would be told they were going to live with their new mummy and daddy. There they would have everything I dreamt of: someone who loved just them and whose attention did not have to be shared with thirty other demanding little souls.

Even Mrs Peacock's dogs, two rather plump Labradors that I loved, would let any small pair of hands stroke them. So when those smiling couples came, I would will them to choose me. But they never did. What was wrong? I asked myself. Why did no one want me?

A woman came every week to visit me. She had dark hair, red lipstick and always wanted to hug me. She told me she was my real mummy and that soon I was going to live with her, but first she had to find a home that was big enough for both of us. I didn't believe her: there were no new clothes and Mrs Peacock hadn't told me that I was going to live with a new mummy and daddy.

I found out many years later that my mother had refused to sign the necessary release forms for adoption: she wanted her children back, according to the social workers.

'So,' said the policeman, 'you admit you were happy there. While the state was ensuring you were cared for, your mother had five years to get her life back together. Do you want me to read what the social workers said?'

I shook my head. I already knew what was in the report sitting in front of him and what was not. Unsuitable accommodation, drinking problems and an abusive marriage were the reasons given for the state's refusal to return me to her. It did not say that soon after their arrest my father had left, that with no one to turn to my mother was almost destitute. After all, it was not she who was their concern. They had removed her last child.

My mother had lost everyone she loved. But the people who removed me were not interested in that. Their concern was for the baby I was then.

CHAPTER SIX

2008 was the year my nightmares returned.

Night after night I wake, my body soaked in perspiration, my mouth still open from the last scream, the sheets tangled around me — the past and present have collided.

'What is it, Madeleine?' my husband asks.

'What is it, Mother?' asks my son.

'What's happening to you?' asks my bewildered thirteen-year-old daughter.

I tell them little bits at a time.

The anger they express at what happened is mixed with disillusion at my having excluded them from my secrets. I understand that, behind their rage, there is a sorrow so enervating it saps the concern from my husband and the love from my daughter.

It is my son who holds my hand and takes me to the police station. My son, who has to hear every word that leaves my lips. The questions fired at me, not just from the police but from those who feel betrayed by my years of silence, hammer in my head. Now I cannot remember who asked which one.

***

The police asked enough to bring back the past but, even worse, they – as others had many years earlier – expressed doubt as to the accuracy of what I told them. They all demanded to know what had happened to me in Haut de la Garenne. I looked at my tormenters one by one until they faded away and the past became more vivid than the present.

What none of them could visualise was what it was like for me on the day when I was taken to that terrible place.

But I could.

It had started as a day like any other. I was in the garden skipping with a rope and singing tunelessly to myself when Mrs Peacock appeared and asked me to come inside. She took me to her room and it was there, sitting in an armchair, impatient to return to my friends, that she told me it was time for me to leave the crèche. 'Madeleine,' she said gently, 'it was your birthday this week. Which one was it?'

'Five,' I said, remembering the cake with its pink icing and the candles I had blown out in one big puff. And the present I was allowed to keep: a blonde-haired doll called Barbie.

'Every little girl wants one of these,' the woman who said to call her 'Mummy' had told me, when she placed it in my hands.

'Five,' Mrs Peacock repeated, 'and what happens, Madeleine, once you are five?'

'I go to school?'

'Yes, you go to school, because you are no longer a little girl, are you?'

'No. I'm a big girl now,' I said proudly, drawing myself up as tall as I could.

'Yes, you are, Madeleine, and this place, the crèche, is for small children. So we have found another place for you, another home, where you will be happy.'

'With a new mummy and daddy?' I asked excitedly.

'No, Madeleine, not yet. It's another place like this but for bigger children.'

I stared at her, uncomprehending. This was my home. It was where my friends were. I knew the name of everyone who looked after us. And was I not Mrs Peacock's favourite? I had overheard a nursery nurse say so. She had said it was no wonder when I had the same colour hair as hers, the strawberry blonde I had inherited from my father, and looked more like her than the woman who visited me.

'No!' I said. 'I won't go.'

Of course I didn't understand that there was nothing she could do. She told me I would make new friends and that I would like school, but nothing she said could pacify me.

'I want to go and live with my other mummy,' I shouted, 'if you don't want me.' My face red with hurt and anger, tears streaming down shiny cheeks, I placed clenched fists on small hips and glared at her.

Instead of being angry she reached for me, pulled me tight into her soft warmth and, while she held me, I cried and cried. Only when my sobs had reduced to snivels did she release me.

'Your mummy cannot have you back yet,' she said. 'But she is looking for a bigger place to live. And she will still visit you every week.' But, by then, neither of us believed that my mother would ever be able to provide a home for her children.

The next day I was bundled into Mrs Peacock's green Morris Minor. Clutching my new doll, I sat in the back. I was leaving everything and everyone I loved. I pressed my face to the window, just watching the countryside slide past. We slowed, turned into a driveway, and then I saw the place that was going to be my new home. A huge, forbidding granite building. The car stopped. I was lifted out.

'Take my hand, Madeleine,' Mrs Peacock told me and, trusting her, I curled my fingers around hers as we walked to the door.

CHAPTER SEVEN

A tall thin man carrying a clipboard ushered us in. Behind him was a warden, for that was what they were called, a slight woman, neither young nor old, with wispy, mousy hair caught back in a bun. He said she would look after me. I noticed a dark mole just under her nose and that her lipstick had leaked into the fine smoker's lines around her mouth. I thought she looked like a witch and tried to move closer to Mrs Peacock.

The man smiled, introduced himself as Mr Tilbrook's deputy, and said that I was to be taken to meet him straight away.

'This is Madeleine's,' said Mrs Peacock, placing a small case on the floor. I knew what was inside it for I had helped pack it. There were the clothes for me to wear to school, my favourite hair ribbons and my doll. I had held her on the journey but just before we had arrived Mrs Peacock had said that she would be safer packed away. 'It's just for a short time, Madeleine,' she had added reassuringly. So I had wrapped her in my newest jumper, a pretty Fair Isle one, kissed the top of her head and told her that she would not be in that dark place for long.

'I'll take that. She can have it later,' the man said, and beckoned to the woman with the dark mole. 'Better that she gets into our routine straight away,' he said to Mrs Peacock. 'Miss Potts here will take her to meet the headmaster. Once Mr Tilbrook has seen her, she will be shown around before meeting some of the other children. I'm sure she'll soon make friends. Now, Madeleine, say goodbye to Mrs Peacock.'

With my mouth trembling, I looked up into the kind face I knew so well. Before I had a chance to cling to the woman who had brought me up since I was a baby and beg her not to leave me there, a firm hand grasped my shoulder and I was whisked away.

The woman who walked me down the long, dark corridors, with grey slate floors and stark, bare walls steeped in the institutional smell I came to hate (that mixture of disinfectant, cheap soap, sweat and despair), informed me that, now I was five, I was no longer a baby. I had to learn that this place did not exist to pamper children. There were rules that to be obeyed and those I had to learn.

The first one was that I was only to speak when spoken to.

The female wardens were to be addressed as 'miss'.

I was to call Mr Tilbrook 'sir' at all times.

'Do you understand, Madeleine?'

'Yes,' I whispered, feeling butterflies wriggling in my stomach.

'Yes, miss,' she corrected me.

We reached a door. She knocked, a man's voice bade us enter and I was in the headmaster's office. It was a large, airy room with two windows overlooking the front of the house and a massive fireplace at the far end. Near the window was his large, wooden desk.

Unlike Mrs Peacock's, with its coloured files, framed photographs and a flowering potted plant, it was bare, except for a long, slender cane. I soon came to know why it was there. He sat behind the desk, unsmiling, a darkly bearded man, dressed in black. That first sight of Colin Tilbrook, whose name I would remember long after he was dead, is ingrained on my memory. He said little to me that day, just repeated what the warden had told me. With no smile or warmth, he stated that I was going to start school and I had to get used to discipline.

This was my first step in growing up. He expected me to obey the rules. He also repeated the instruction that I must call him 'sir' and the female wardens 'miss'. 'Do you understand?'

'Yes,' I mumbled. As I looked into his eyes I saw a cold darkness in them that made me shudder.

'Yes, what, Madeleine?'

'Yes, sir.'

That was my first lesson.

He dismissed me then, saying he would see me on another day when I had settled in, and told the warden to show me where I had to go.

I was marched down more dark corridors to a room, Miss Potts said, where all the stores were kept. Inside, shelves overflowed with clothes, towels and bedding. It was, she added, kept locked at all times. Only the wardens had the key.

I was mystified as to why she had told me that, and why we were there. After all, I had everything I needed with me and I tried to tell her so. She ignored my stumbling words, told me to be quiet and that she was too busy to listen to a little girl's prattle. Without another word, she pulled item after item off the shelves and piled them into my arms – a grey pinafore dress, grey underwear and two nightdresses. My arms ached as I followed her into the dormitory, with its two rows of metal-framed white beds and small, battered lockers.

I was told to place a nightdress at the bottom of the bed and everything else in the locker.

Next she showed me the bathrooms, with their rows of basins, gave me a toothbrush, a tin of pink paste, a flannel and a comb. I was too frightened by then to tell her I already had those things. Instead I obediently placed them in the drawstring bag she handed me and hung it on a hook.

The rest of that day is a blur – the dining room with long tables and wooden benches where children sat in enforced silence, the greasy food that made me feel sick, but the very worst was bedtime, at which the mousy-haired woman officiated.

'Where are my things? My case? My doll is in it!'

'You will wear the clothes that are given to you,' she snapped.

'But my doll,' I pleaded.

'Dolls,' she said firmly, 'are for babies and you are no longer a baby.'

With a sinking heart, I understood that I was not going to see my doll again, or wear my pretty Fair Isle jumper, or have my hair tied back in those bright ribbons. The case, with my precious things, was lost to me.

In bed, I drew my knees to my chest, placed my thumb in my mouth and sobbed myself to sleep.

CHAPTER EIGHT

It was always a boy who came for me. 'Mr Tilbrook wants to see you, Madeleine,' was all he said each time.

My throat would close with fear as I clenched my hands. I wanted to put my fingers in my ears, blocking out the boy's voice. Each time those thoughts raced through my head, a warden would glance in my direction.

'What are you sitting there for, Madeleine? You heard what was said to you so off you go. You mustn't keep Sir waiting, must you?'

I ignored the looks that came my way from the other children, some pitying, others relieved that this time it was me he had sent for, and a few gleeful, from those who took pleasure in seeing fear on small children's faces.

The first time he sent for me I was scared that I must have done something wrong and was going to be punished. To my surprise, when I went into his office, he did not look angry. The frown he wore when patrolling the corridors had been replaced with a smile.

'That will be all,' he said to my escort, and motioned me to come around the desk to where he was sitting.

'Well, Madeleine, how are you settling in?' he asked, the moment the door closed behind the boy.

I opened my mouth to speak, but the words stuck in my throat. My legs were shaking and the butterflies in my stomach were fluttering again.

'Come now, Madeleine, look at me when I'm speaking to you, not at the floor.' A finger went under my chin.

I didn't like his face: all that hair and eyes so dark they seemed like mirrors where I could see my reflection. His hand stroked my hair. A sweet appeared and some of my fear left me.

'Come,' he said and, sitting back, he lifted me up and sat me on his knee. 'Now, Madeleine, we're going to be friends, aren't we?'

I nodded. I wanted to please him.

His hand started stroking my leg. Fingers slid around my ankle, then travelled upwards. Dark hair sprouted from them and, as I stared in horror, his hand seemed to become a huge spider, which was crawling over me.

I wanted to leap off his lap and run to the door, but there was nowhere for me to go. No nice nursery nurse would comfort me and wrap her arms around me. There was just him and the hard-faced wardens.

The spider climbed higher, went between my legs and one finger slipped under my knickers' elastic. I might have been only five, but that place was private! It was for peeing and I didn't want it touched. But fear made me sit completely still.

Of course, as I grew from childhood to adulthood, I learnt that over the centuries there have always been men who have raped, tortured and murdered women and little girls because they were spoils of war, because they were their possessions or just because they could. And, as I was to discover, there were also women in the world who were the very opposite of the warm, caring mother figures I had encountered in my earlier years. But then I still believed that grown-ups were there to protect us, to bandage cut knees and read us bedtime stories.

I had also been told, for as long as I could understand, that adults were to be obeyed. So when he moved me onto his chair and told me to close my eyes and not open them until he said I could, I obeyed him.

When he forced my mouth open and pushed something hot and sour between my lips, I didn't move.

And when my face was covered in something hot and sticky, I still sat there rigidly.

His voice, hoarser than before, told me I was a good girl and that I could open my eyes. He moved to wipe my face with his handkerchief, but the smell of something like bleach, combined with the fear that his action had generated, made my stomach churn and, without warning, I vomited. My fingers went up to my mouth as the hot stream spurted from it.

With an exclamation of disgust he shoved the waste-paper bin towards me and told me not to miss. I was beyond caring about his annoyance as, eyes streaming, I bent double and retched and retched.

I have no memory of how I got back to the room where the other children were.

Much later, I lay in my cold, hard bed, my arms curled tightly around my knees, trying to make myself as small as possible, while tears trickled down my face.

***

The next day I started school.

CHAPTER NINE

A voice, loud and harsh, entered my dreams, making my eyes spring open and my body clench with fear. Above me loomed the face of the warden who had opened the door the day I had arrived. The one who had taken my doll and all my pretty things. This time the conciliatory smile had been replaced by an expression that I saw, blinking with the residue of an uneasy sleep, was far from friendly.

'Get out of bed now,' she was saying. 'Seven o'clock and still sleeping, Madeleine, on your first day at school, too.' She threw my blankets and sheets onto the floor. I tried to say sorry, but before I was able to utter the word, her arm snaked out and she jerked me off the mattress to land in a heap on the floor by my bedding. 'And here I was thinking you would be one of the first up. Surely this is an exciting day for you, isn't it?'

I didn't feel excited, only scared. Those treacherous butterflies were swarming in my stomach, and my tongue felt as though it was glued to the roof of my mouth. I swallowed, then remembered what had been instilled in me and quickly muttered 'Yes, miss.'

'Well, I'm sure you know what it means when you start school, don't you?' Without waiting for a reply she gave me a mocking smile. 'It means you're a big girl, and what do big girls do, Madeleine?'

Not knowing what answer she wanted I just gulped and stared at her.

'They make their beds, Madeleine. And when it is done to my satisfaction, they get their breakfast. Now, I have already done half your work, stripped your bed for you, haven't I? So what do you say?'

I could feel the eyes of every girl in that dormitory looking at me. My legs shook, I wanted to wee and, more than anything, I wanted Mrs Peacock.

'Thank you, miss,' whispered a dark-haired girl, who looked about thirteen, standing at the foot of the bed next to me.

'Thank you, miss,' I repeated.

The warden glared at my rescuer. 'Well, Frances, since you're so good at speaking for Madeleine, you can show her how to make her bed, as well as your own. You'll have to be extra fast, mind. You know what happens to girls who are late for breakfast, don't you?'

'They don't get any, miss.'

'That's right, Frances. They don't get any. So you had better start now.' She marched to the door where, with a glance over her shoulder, she added, 'I'll be back as soon as I've had my morning cup of tea, so get started, girls.'

It was not until her steps faded that Frances spoke. 'Come on, Madeleine, give me a hand. We want to spoil her fun, don't we? That rotten cow really gets off on sending girls out for the day with an empty stomach. So let's make sure it doesn't happen to us.' To my relief, her mischievous grin sliced through any annoyance she might have felt at being given a double workload.

'Sheets first,' she told me, tossing the bottom one into the air and letting it float onto the bed. 'These are what we have to get right first, see?' She showed me how to make envelope tucks at the bottom corners. 'Stops your feet sticking out,' she added, as she tucked the rest firmly under the mattress, 'Do you know why that's important?'

I shook my head.

'If the night warden sees a bare foot she hits them with a torch. So unless you want to hobble for a week, make sure the sheets are firmly tucked in. The secret is to pull them tight – any wrinkles and that cow makes us do it again.'

Deftly she pulled and tucked until both beds were finished. 'Now we stand and wait for the inspection,' she said.

No sooner had we placed ourselves by the beds than the warden was back. She walked up and down, letting some girls go and stopping at others, where she voiced her displeasure and yanked off their bedding. It was a regular occurrence.

'Remake it and this time make sure you do it properly,' she snapped, before continuing on to the next. Three girls were told to remake their beds. Their shoulders slumped when they heard the words. They knew there would be no breakfast for them.

Oh, please say ours are all right, I repeated in my head, as I watched the warden go from bed to bed. I was hungry and the thought of having nothing to eat until lunchtime made me feel dizzy.

'Mmm,' the warden said, when she finally came to us. 'You're learning fast, Madeleine, but I think you had a little help. Maybe tomorrow I'd better watch you and make sure you're doing everything yourself,' she added, with a malicious smirk. 'Now you'd better go and get washed before you get dressed. Off you go.'

Needing no encouragement, we raced to the bathrooms, splashed water on our faces and brushed our teeth, with the horrible pink paste, then rushed back to our lockers and scrambled into our clothes.

It was my hair that was the problem. It was still long and I had been told that I must have it tied back for school. Seeing my futile efforts, Frances seized the brush, ran it through my curls, then fixed them into a ponytail.

'All done, Madeleine,' she told me, but her wide smile failed to wipe out the memory of Colin Tilbrook's office and what had happened there. Heat scorched my cheeks as it slid into my mind. If Frances wondered why I had looked momentarily disconcerted, she passed no comment.

'No time for plaits,' she said. 'Let's hope no one decides that's what they want. Now, come on, you'll miss breakfast often enough, but not on your first day at school, kid.' She squeezed my hand, then pulled me after her, down one flight of stairs and up another, into what looked like a church hall furnished with wooden benches and tables.

This was my first morning.

Before, I had eaten with the other pre-schoolers in a much smaller room. What struck me as we entered that hall, which was full of boys and girls of all ages, was the overpowering silence. No one spoke. They queued up for their food quietly, took their plates back to the tables and, eyes down, they ate. No talking during meals I had been told, but it was the first time I had experienced it.

This time, unlike the other days when I longed for the coddled eggs that I had had at the crèche, I gobbled down the lumpy porridge and cold toast. The knowledge that it had almost been denied me made it more appetising. Hardly had I swallowed my last mouthful than the bell rang. It was time to meet in the hall and be taken to our schools.

A warden I had not met before was escorting the younger children. Unlike the ones I had already met, she was friendly. Although the years have eroded her name, I remembered that she asked me mine, introduced herself, smiled warmly and told me I was going to enjoy school. It turned out she was in charge of the younger children. 'I've been on holiday,' she said, explaining why we had not met before. She was the first person in authority I had met who seemed kind and I wished that she was the one inspecting our beds. I was sure she would see that my hands were too small to make it up by myself.

'Now, Madeleine,' she said, as we walked in the direction of the school, 'I know that you're the only one who is starting today, but here are the twins, who are only a year ahead of you.' She called two little girls to her side. 'Mandy and Ann,' she said, 'this is Madeleine, and I want to hear later that in the breaks you looked after her. You remember what it was like on your first day, don't you? Though I am sure it won't take Madeleine long to make friends. You'll do that for me, won't you?'

'Yes, miss,' they piped, and two pairs of brown eyes in round freckled faces looked into mine and two rosebud mouths smiled at me. I wondered why I hadn't met them earlier.

Later I found out that they had been chosen for adoption and, as soon as the formalities were finished with, they would be leaving Haut de la Garenne. While they were waiting to go to their new home they had been left in the younger children's section.

'Good. So you won't be alone at playtime, Madeleine.'

I remembered what Mrs Peacock had told me – that school was where I would make friends.

Once we arrived at the pale grey building, I was handed over to a teacher, who seemed more preoccupied with greeting the parents than taking any notice of me. All around there were well-dressed young mothers with small children clutching their hands. Little faces turned up to receive a flurry of kisses, 'Darling, enjoy your first day,' and little waves. A last word to the teacher and assurances that the mothers would be there to meet their children as soon as the last bell rang: that was what I remembered, as I stood there alone.

When the parents had left, some brushing away a tear, the teacher ushered us into the classroom, which was light and airy, the walls decorated with pictures of stick figures wearing bright clothes. I cannot remember what we did that first morning. But I do remember the snub-nosed boy I sat next to. 'Please, miss,' he said, 'I don't want to sit next to her. My mummy told me not to mix with naughty children.'

The teacher looked at him over her glasses. 'Well, Alan,' she said, 'there is no other seat, and Madeleine is not naughty. She is just not as fortunate as you. Now, enough of this nonsense. And on your first day, too.'

I heard muffled giggles, felt glances coming my way and, with burning cheeks, I studied the top of my desk, wondering miserably if she would have been so firm if there had been another empty seat.

Break came, and I watched other children playing. School, I had been told, was where big girls made new friends. But no little girl came up to me. Where were Mandy and Ann? They, I discovered later, had been kept in. Someone had thrown a ball of paper. 'It's always us who get the blame,' they told me.

It was, in fact, as I was to learn, anyone who was at Haut de la Garenne.

'Naughty kid! You are a naughty kid!' yelled my classmates, when we were outside.

I watched Alan with his friends. He seemed bigger than the other children. Dressed in grey shorts with a blue blazer over a crisp white shirt, he strutted in front of me. 'Naughty girl,' he sang, while I looked at the ground.

Mrs Peacock had been wrong. School was not where big girls made new friends.

CHAPTER TEN

2008

I was in a room devoid of furniture. Against the glass walls, twisted branches of a bare tree tapped a stark message. 'Get out, get out, Madeleine,' they were telling me. Where was the door? I had to find it. I needed to escape. I could feel a malevolence, an invisible force in there with me.

My hands pressed against the cold glass, and it was then I saw, beneath the tree, people gathering. Faces turned up, steamy wisps of rising breath, mouths moving.

I couldn't hear the words, just feel the waves of fury directed at me.

'Move,' I told myself. 'Move where they can't see you.' But a cold, damp fog wrapped itself around my limbs, pinning me to the spot.

One man, seeing my small figure, raised his fist and shook it. As though that was the signal they had been waiting for, the crowd of men, women and children rushed forward, their clenched fists proclaiming their hatred. The sound of breathing behind me made my spine twitch with fear. Someone had got in. It was too late.

Slowly I turned and I started to cry.

A wet nose nuzzled my side. It was Joey, one of Mrs Peacock's Labradors. As my hand moved to stroke him he changed, in front of my terrified eyes, from my old friend, with the warm soulful eyes, into something quite different: a demonic creature with foam-flecked lips curled back over yellow teeth. Coat bristling, a growl rumbling deep in his throat, eyes tinged with red – and, dangling between his legs, a huge red thing.

Oh, God! It was going to attack me with it. 'No, no, no,' I whimpered, pressing myself harder against the glass. Outside I saw, with a clutch of fear, that people, their eyes fixed on the windows, were climbing the trees. I knew that once they got to the top they would break the glass and come in. My head turned as I searched desperately for escape, but there was nowhere to run to, nowhere to hide. Then, as I heard the glass breaking, Joey sprang.

I was screaming. My arms thrashed, my feet kicked and then a terrible pain shot through them.

'Mum, what is it?' A soft hand touched my shoulder. 'Wake up, Mum. It's only a bad dream.'

Groggily, I opened my eyes. My two children were there, concern stamped on their faces. A hot drink was made for me, my sheets smoothed and my pillows plumped. 'It was only a dream, Mum,' my daughter said.

But it wasn't. It was the one I thought had finally left me.

The one I had had when I was five.

The memory of that first time came flooding back. My small five-year-old self, throat constricted with fear, clutching her bedclothes, looking up into the cold gaze of the warden. My five-year-old self had not been woken by gentle hands or given a warm drink before being tucked back into bed. And the adult me wanted to weep for her.

'What do you think you're doing, making such a disturbance, Madeleine?' a woman's voice had asked.

I was shaking as I woke, the tail end of my night terror still lingering, and looked into the dazzling white light of a torch. It was grasped in the hand of the warden – and the pain I had felt in my foot was the remembered pain of the frightened five-year-old who had been struck by the warden's torch.

'Out you get, Madeleine,' she had said. 'You know what happens to children who wake everyone up.'

I crawled out of the bed on wobbly legs. I knew what the punishment was for making any sound after the lights were out: standing in the corridor for as long as the warden left us.

I felt the dampness of my nightgown at the same moment as the warden saw the tell-tale wet patch. 'Look what you've done, you disgusting little girl. You've wet yourself. Well, you'll have to wash your sheets in the morning. I'm not looking for clean ones now. You'll just have to keep that stinking nightdress of yours on until then as well. Now, out you go. You can stand in that corridor until I say you can get back into bed.'

Her hand took hold of my arm, the tender part above my elbow. Her fingers dug in, making me wince, as she dragged me out of the dormitory into the dimly lit corridor. 'You can stand here until I come back for you. No sitting on the floor or leaning against the wall either. Do you hear me, Madeleine?'

'Yes, miss,' I whispered.

The corridor was dark. A faint light from the staff-room cast shadows, which, in my befuddled head, became shapes shifting and creeping towards me. I stood there shivering, my damp nightdress clinging to my body, my foot throbbing. My head nodded, my eyes closed . . . then, with a start, I jerked awake. Just when I thought I couldn't stand any longer, that I would be unable to stop myself sliding to the ground, she appeared. 'Right, Madeleine, you can get back into your smelly bed now.'

I crawled in, tried to curl my body away from the damp patch. It seemed that no sooner had I fallen asleep than I was being shaken awake. This time, when I opened my eyes, instead of the warden's face it was Frances's.

'Come, Madeleine,' she said gently. 'Let's get you cleaned up and your sheet washed. That fucking bitch told me that as I'd helped you the first time I could do it again.'

Tears leaked out of my eyes. It was the kindness underneath her rough tone that made me want to sob. Her hand brushed my face. 'Don't cry, Madeleine, we haven't got time. You'll just have to be brave a little longer.'

Outside, the moon had faded to a pale lemon crescent while streaks of red showed in the almost black sky. In the dusky dimness of the hour between night and morning, we stumbled to the laundry room. There, we scrubbed the sheets by hand and hung them on the wooden clothes horse that Frances pulled down from the ceiling by its rope.

'Arms up,' she said to me, once the clothes horse had been hauled back up. She pulled my nightdress over my shoulders. I stood there meekly while she helped me into my clothes and did my hair. Then she put her arm around me and gave me a little squeeze. 'Why are you here?' she asked. 'I've seen you have visitors. Is there no one outside who could take you?'

'My mummy,' I said. 'I'm just waiting for her to find us a home.'

'Well, then, I'm sure she will.'

CHAPTER ELEVEN

My being a well-behaved child at school ended a week later, just after the Monday when I nearly missed supper.

I was sitting in the common room when a boy came in. 'Madeleine,' he said, with no effort to keep his voice down, 'Mr Tilbrook wants to see you in his office.'

I felt everyone looking at me and my face burned with shame. They knew, I thought. They knew about that horrible thing he kept in his trousers. They all knew what he made me do with it.

My fingers clenched the sides of my chair. I didn't want to go.

'Run along, Madeleine,' said an adult voice.

Without looking up, I knew which warden it was: the one who smirked whenever I was sent for. My hands lost their grip. I knew I had no choice. I stood up and followed the boy to Mr Tilbrook's office.

A licentious smile, a brush on my arm, a taking hold of my fingers, a quickly muttered, 'Good little girl,' and Colin Tilbrook was ready for me.

Maybe it was being called 'good' by Mr Tilbrook that made me decide I no longer wanted to be good. Maybe it was because I was so tired. Maybe it was because my nightmares didn't come only when I was asleep.

Whichever it was, that was the beginning of me antagonising my teacher. At school, too often, my eyes could hardly stay open.

'Madeleine, pay attention,' the teacher kept repeating, a note of exasperation creeping into her voice. When she asked the class to recite a nursery rhyme, one that I had often heard, I was the only one who couldn't get it right.

'Oh, Madeleine, you've heard that so many times,' she said. 'I don't think you're trying today. Now,' she said brightly, 'can anyone tell me what story I read to you yesterday?'

Alan's hand was the first to shoot up, quickly followed by the rest of the class. I alone sat with mine in my lap. 'It was about Jack and Jill, miss.'

'Indeed it was, Alan. Very good.'

He smirked, more at my discomfort than her praise, I knew.

Pictures were held up. A for apple but the letter was blurred, as was the next one: B for banana. 'D?' I said hopefully, when asked, and another sigh left the teacher's mouth.

'Madeleine, it's the letter after A.'

Simple arithmetic was no better. 'Two times two, Madeleine?' she asked, but all I could see in my head was a jumble of numbers.

'Stupid,' hissed Alan, and tears flooded my eyes.

It was during break that anger suddenly replaced fear. 'Stupid girl, stupid girl,' my tormentor sang as, to the merriment of his admirers, he circled me. My hand lashed out, caught his shoulder hard, and down he went. His howls, more of outrage than pain, brought the teacher rushing over.

'Madeleine, that was very naughty,' she said.

I was the naughty child after that and put on the naughty chair to prove it.

The next morning I heard Alan's mother talking to the teacher on playground duty. One who looked much sterner than the one in charge of our class. 'Just not right that our children have to mix with these rough children,' she said, indicating our little group.

'I agree with you, but our hands are tied. This is the only school near them. I tell them to leave the other children alone. They can play with each other in the breaks.'

'Yes, I've told my son to keep well away from them after yesterday. Well, they're not in that place for no reason, are they? I mean, look at that child who attacked my son,' she added, nodding in my direction. 'She looks so sweet, doesn't she? As though butter wouldn't melt in her mouth.'

'Yes, but what a temper. I thought she was going to kick me when I pulled her and your boy apart. Completely unprovoked, too. No, she's already a problem. I told her teacher that she needs watching, all right.'

'It was a good thing it was you who was there. That one in charge of their class seems rather soft to me.'

They must have felt my eyes on them for they suddenly ceased talking and stared at me. What I saw reflected in their eyes made me want to curl up and disappear. Instead, I looked straight back at them.

'No shame,' said the mother.

They were wrong.

That was the day when I came to believe that the only reason I was at Haut de la Garenne was because I had done something bad. The only problem was that I simply could not remember what it was.

CHAPTER TWELVE

Each day when school ended, there was the nice warden, ready to collect us. The highlight of my day was the walk, where she chatted to me until we reached the home. If school bored and depressed me, then so did Haut de la Garenne. I had been used to a large garden to play in, friendly carers wiping small hands before teatime, warm baths and bedtime stories before the lights were turned out so I found the regimental routine suffocating and oppressive.

It was a regime Colin Tilbrook ran with a military precision that he and the wardens enforced by browbeating and bullying. We didn't dare to disobey them, or ignore the bells, much as we wanted to. Fear was instilled in us from the moment we walked through those doors. Worse, beyond fear, apathy set in once we had accepted the behaviour of those in control. Within a matter of days most of the younger children became cowed, nervous little creatures, who knew that any moment someone was going to hurt them. But there was something in me, even then, that refused to give up. I snatched moments of happiness whenever I could and dreamt of leaving that place.

The routine at the home seldom varied.

On our return from school, coats were hung up, bags placed in lockers and we were free to play, but not for long. In no time at all the bell was ringing to summon us for our five o'clock supper. An unappetising meal it might have been, but it was the only one until breakfast, so every scrap was eaten. Once we had cleared away the dishes and been given permission to leave the dining hall, we made our way back to the common room.

There, we were allowed to amuse ourselves for less than an hour, for at six o'clock the wardens, eager to finish work, marched all of us younger children to the bathrooms. Leaning against the walls, they watched as we brushed teeth, washed hands and faces and pulled on night clothes. As soon as we were ready, we were marched to the dormitories and clambered into bed. Lights were turned off promptly at six thirty, although a dim light in the corridor was kept on.

The older children, who had homework to complete, were left to their studies, and often we were asleep before they came in.

'No talking,' the stern-faced wardens told us every night. 'You know what happens if we have to come in, don't you? You disturb us, and you'll find yourselves standing in that corridor for so long that you'll wish you were asleep.' Faced with that threat we lay stiffly, the sheets pulled up to our chests.

Of course, not being sleepy, we were tempted to whisper, but each time that happened, the perpetrator was caught. Those wardens must have crept along the corridors, held a glass to the walls or had extrasensory perception, for they would suddenly appear, claiming they had heard us talking.

In bed, engulfed in sadness, my thumb would slide into my mouth. I had been told that only babies did that, but I needed comfort. Every night I would curl up tightly and hold my breath as I listened for the night warden's footsteps. When I heard them I prayed that nothing about me would draw her attention.

I tried to stay awake, but what if, in my sleep, my feet showed through the bedding? There would be that terrible pain again. Or if I had another nightmare and cried out in my sleep? Then I would be made to stand on that dark, cold landing. Even worse, what if my dreams tormented me so badly that I wet myself again?

No, I couldn't bear it.

The air around me was full of small sounds. The deep breathing of those lucky enough to be sleeping peacefully and the small moans of those who were not.

There were other sounds, which, then, I didn't understand. Footsteps tiptoeing into the dormitory, a startled cry of protest, a voice deeper than those of the wardens, uttering indistinguishable words. There was menace in its tone and desperation in the cries. On hearing that, I tucked my head under the blanket. I didn't want to see the shadowy form, holding a pillow, creeping past me. I knew who it was but not then what they wanted.

Lying there in the dark, I tried to picture something happy, something I could lose myself in. Anything that would transport me away from that terrible place. With my eyes squeezed tightly shut, I took myself back to days when the sun shone, children laughed and I was happy.

Behind my eyelids I could see smiling faces . . . faces that grew dimmer as the weeks passed and my memories, like old photographs, began to fade. But there was one that I refused to let go. I made it float in my mind until I almost felt I was there.

It was my special day. I had been chosen to present a bouquet of flowers to a lady I had been told was important. Who she was, I don't remember. But I do recollect very clearly that I was at an event held at the Opera House. Even more importantly, I had brand new clothes to wear. A pink dress and matching shoes. All morning, nearly sick with excitement, I had practised and practised my curtsy.

'You'll walk beside me, Madeleine,' Mrs Peacock had told me. 'Then just a few steps on your own, before you bend your knee into a curtsy, and as you come up, you hand the lady the flowers.'

That day I left my friends playing and was whisked away to be got ready. First a bath, then I was sat, wrapped in a fluffy white towel, on Mrs Peacock's knee, as my hair was rubbed dry then brushed. How content I was then to lean against her and feel her arms around me. I just wanted to nestle up, inhale the familiar scent of soap and face powder and listen to her voice. I wished then, as I had so often, that she was my mother and that I could live with her and her big, friendly dogs.

In those daydreams I still played with my friends at the crèche, still had the wet noses of dogs nuzzling, but at night I went to a proper home. There I would have my own bedroom and the toys in it would be mine. And in her house her time would belong to me alone.

'Come, don't fall asleep here,' she had said, laughing, as she stood me gently on the floor. 'Time for you to put on that lovely new dress, Madeleine,' she told me, as she helped me into my underwear. I felt the pink dress slither over my shoulders and her fingers buttoning it up.

My toes wriggled into white socks, new shoes buckled, a tug of my hem, a smoothing of my collar, and she was satisfied. 'Now don't you look pretty?' she said, as, with one hand on my shoulder, we stood in front of a mirror.

I stared at the reflection of a slight green-eyed girl with strawberry blonde hair and a scattering of freckles over her nose. I smiled. She was right. I did look pretty.

'Pleased?' she asked.

I murmured that I was.

The next picture of that day was when I was on the stage. I had walked on with Mrs Peacock. She let go of my hand and I took those last few steps alone. My fingers clasped the bouquet tightly and the words, 'Bend your knee into a curtsy, and as you come up, you hand the lady the flowers,' sounded in my head.

The lady gave me a wide smile when she bent down to take the flowers in a gloved hand and kissed my cheek. 'Thank you, Madeleine,' she said, as though my appearing in front of her was a huge surprise.

That she knew my name was the best part. Each time I summoned up those images, the longing to be back at the crèche intensified, but then, as the weeks passed, other feelings arose. Resentment of those in power, sorrow for what I had lost and a sense of unworthiness.

I didn't understand why children left the crèche at five, or know that my mother didn't want me adopted, so I began to believe that I was unwanted.

CHAPTER THIRTEEN

2008

I was not, I had told the police, going to talk only about the Jordans. There was more, so much more.

With their questions, they had prised open the box in which every therapist tells damaged patients to store their bad memories. The one in the corner of the mind's storeroom. In mine, the ghosts of murdered childhoods had slumbered for nearly forty years.

I was twenty when I slammed down the lid on those pictures of suffering, never to look at them again, as I told myself when I started my new life – a life in which my past had been washed clean. Now they clawed at my mind, crept into my dreams, slid into my subconscious and haunted even my waking hours. It was as though all those years of creating a new self, all those years of silence, had been for nothing.

So, in stages, I told my story to my son. He wrote it down and delivered it to the police. And they sent for me, turned on their tape recorders and fired their rehearsed questions. And I let them know that it was the whole story I wanted told, not just a fragment.

They were, I thought, intent on bringing two people back from Scotland to punish them for their crimes. Two people who were undeniably evil. But surely the police were now going to investigate the others. All right, some of them were dead, but what difference should that make? I and others wanted them named and their memories shamed.

The question we began to ask was: 'What about the ones who came from the island? Are their names to be left untarnished? Their deeds hidden so that Jersey can retain its image of being the millionaires' nirvana?'

No. It would be the whole story or nothing.

Another interview: the same policeman, a different woman.

'Now, Madeleine, you informed us that in the July of 1966 you saw a boy hanging from a tree. That it was a suicide. And you know why he did it. Is that right?'

'Yes, I remember very clearly seeing him dangling in the tree.'

'And, at the age of six, you knew why he had done it?'

'No, not then, but later I did.'

'All right, we'll come to what led you to be so convinced that it was suicide and not just some boyish prank gone wrong later. First, though, I have a few more questions for you. I have to be truthful here. I find this part of your statement very difficult to believe.

Oh, I'm not saying you're deliberately giving us false information. I think you're convinced that everything you tell us is the truth. But, in all honesty, we are not. I mean it was, what? Forty-one years ago? And you were still only six.' He picked up some notes, glanced at them, then carefully placed them back on his desk. 'Now, what concerns me about the validity of this particular statement is, according to what we know, you were unable to either read or write. So you could not have recorded those events in some secret little diary now, could you?'

I looked up at him, trying not to let my anger show. 'No, but something as shocking as that stays in your mind, doesn't it? I'd never seen someone dead before.'

'Yes, I understand that. But, Madeleine, let's be honest here. There are other factors to take into account, such as why your memory might not be as reliable as you think.'

'It's not something I could forget,' I said, before he had a chance to bring up the other factors. 'However many years have passed makes no difference. After all, it was my friends and I who found him.'

'And that, you say, was in the July of 1966. The thirtieth, to be exact,' he said, fixing me with another of his penetrating stares. 'You are certain of that date and

I find that, well, puzzling, to say the least. You couldn't even tell the time then, far less read a calendar. That is the truth, isn't it?' he said, leaning back on his chair.

I smiled then, as I knew he thought he had scored enough points on this interview to discredit my statement. So I kept quiet and waited for his next question, the one I knew was coming.

'So, Madeleine, tell us what makes you so sure of not just the year but the month and the day as well?'

'It was the year England won the World Cup,' I said, failing to keep some degree of triumph from my voice. 'That's why I know when it was. I looked it up much later so I could put a date on it.'.

'You remember the World Cup?' he said, with a grin. 'You were following the matches, then?'

'No, I was interested in the fact that, for once, the wardens were ignoring us.'

'All right, then. So let's go over how you found him. I thought you were all pretty much supervised in that place, not allowed much freedom. Well, that's what you've been telling me.'

'As I just said, the wardens were ignoring us. It was the final. They and the boys, the big ones, were crowded together in front of the television. Our group went up to see what was so interesting and we were told to go away. Said we were too young and, anyhow, there was no space for us. That was how come we were free to go out into the grounds to play,' I told him, with some exasperation, as my mind slid back through the decades to that day.

One of the girls had found a skipping rope and, giddy with the unexpected freedom, we picked it up and ran giggling outside. Two of the children were swinging the rope and I began jumping over it.

'You know,' I said, looking at the officer, 'what was sad about that day was that, for once, we were just little girls playing, with no other thoughts in our minds but enjoying our freedom. And then it all changed. Sarah, who'd only just come to Haut de la Garenne, suddenly let out a piercing shriek.'

And once again I was back in that field, feeling that tingle of fear, as my eyes followed the direction of her pointing finger.

'What's the matter?' we had asked, looking down the field.

'There's something dangling in that tree. What is it?'

It was sunny that day and I'd squinted, trying to see. 'It's a boy,' I said. 'What's he doing?' We all looked at each other then, and the skin on my arms was prickling as we slowly walked towards that tree.

'When we reached it,' I said to the policeman, 'we all stood looking up at something they told us had never been there. But it had. Can you imagine how terrifying that was for all of us?'

It was a question he chose not to answer as my mind replayed those events.

Before we got there we kept trying to tell ourselves that it was a game, just some boy trying to frighten us. After all, they were always playing pranks on us younger ones. But standing underneath him, we knew that something dreadful had happened. His head was bent sideways, but it was his eyes we couldn't tear our gaze from. They were red, so red it was as though his blood was seeping out of them.

As young as we were, we knew he was never going to pull the rope off his neck, swing up onto the branch, laugh and yell, 'Got yer!' before bursting into wild laughter.

Other details came into focus as I spoke to the police. How I had seen that the crotch of his trousers was stained with piss, and my nose was twitching as I smelt him. He had shat himself as he died, that boy. That boy of only ten.

I think now of just how scared he must have been of his life at the home to leave it in that way.

'Did we try to lift him by his legs? I'd like to think we did, but my memory's blank as to what happened next. I have no recollection of us leaving the field.

Just of being back in the house, screaming, crying and shouting.'

'What happened then?'

I told them that the wardens had torn themselves from the black and white picture on the screen and rushed out. Our group was swiftly taken into another room before we had a chance to tell anyone else what we had seen. It was one of the female wardens who sat us down and talked to us. For once, kind words came in our direction while we sat tearfully in front of her.

I remember her saying she was getting us a drink that would calm us down and each of us was given a glass half full of some dark liquid, which we were told to swallow straight down. It burnt my throat making me splutter, but I felt my body start to relax as the warmth hit my stomach.

'Now I know you've seen something that distressed you,' the warden said, 'but it's best if you don't talk about it. Do you understand?'

We might not have understood why, but we recognised a command when we heard one and nodded.

'But something must have happened after that?' This time it was the policewoman who spoke. 'I mean, surely you must have been given some explanation, if what you say is correct?'

'The only other reference to the whole incident that I can recall was all of us being ordered into the big hall where we had our meals,' I replied. '"An unfortunate incident" was how Colin Tilbrook referred to a boy's death before leading us in prayers. And that was the end of it. It was never mentioned again by any of the staff.'

'A boy hanged himself, a terrible thing, but sadly a few messed up kids do that.'

I forced myself to appear calm, as I waited for the policeman to elaborate on his remarks.

'Could have been any number of reasons that he did it,' he went on. 'Even, as I said before, a prank that went wrong. I just don't know how a little girl of six would know what his reason was.'

'I have another memory of that boy,' I said. 'A very clear one. There was a man who came to the home. A man who liked little boys. He was a friend of Colin Tilbrook's. I saw the boy with him.'

'And?' he said impatiently.

'We all knew, even us little ones, what the men who came to the home wanted,' I replied.

As I spoke, the picture of what I had seen came into my mind, not blurred and faded as old snaps are, but as sharp and clear as though it had just been taken. With my eyes half closed I looked at it, careful that I described every detail exactly as I had seen it that day.

The man had his back to me. His belt was undone, his trousers were around his knees, and I could see those pale, flabby buttocks quivering. One hand was against the wall steadying him, his legs were spread and between them I could see another pair. Skinny ones in short trousers.

Then I saw that the man was clutching something with his other hand. It was the top of the boy's head. He was moving that little head back and forward, back and forward, faster and faster, as he quivered and grunted before giving a shout, not of pain but of pleasure.

I knew what he was doing. That thing he kept in his trousers had swollen and it was in the boy's mouth, choking him, making his eyes stream and his stomach churn. I saw the man's body shake, then he zipped up his trousers and pushed the boy away.

He was crying, the boy. His face was red and he was rubbing it with the back of his sleeve when he ran from the room.

The policeman looked up as I finished describing what I had seen. 'Who was the man, Madeleine?'

'I don't know.'

That is what I told those police and, for a few seconds, there was silence in the room.

'How did you know that, Madeleine?' the policeman asked, and from the gentleness that had, for the first time, crept into his voice, I knew the answer was already in his head and he had no wish to hear it. 'How can you remember such detail?'

'Because,' I said, 'that was what Colin Tilbrook made me do every week when he sent for me.'

And I heard my son's sharp intake of breath.

'Were you not frightened, Madeleine? Did you not run out of the room? And which room was it? I mean, he must not have thought he would be seen.'

'I can't remember,' I answered. For, with the telling, the picture slipped away. I could conjure up nothing else.

The policeman made movements to show that the interview was over. As he half rose from his chair he said, but not unkindly, 'Did you ever tell your mother, Madeleine?' 'No,' I said, but I lied.

CHAPTER FOURTEEN

I had told her, not when I left but on one of those days when I had been allowed to visit.

Through the distance of years I saw my six-year-old self, wearing hand-me-down clothes, too large for her small frame, standing in a room where a woman whose eyes were ringed with tiredness was looking at her in shock. All my mother had wanted that day was to make my visit as special as possible.

That morning she had come to fetch me from Haut de la Garenne. One of the wardens had told me that I was to spend the day with her and I was already hovering in the hall when she arrived. For several weeks she had been living with a man she told me was my new stepfather, Frank, a short, stocky Irishman, with a workman's hands and a generous smile.

On my visits he had tried his best to get to know me, but each time I had been struck with a mixture of fear and shyness. He tried to reassure me that the dismal bedsitter would not remain their home for long. 'Your mother and I want to find something nicer,' he had said, the first time I met him. 'One with enough rooms so you can come and live with us. You'd like that, wouldn't you, Madeleine?'

Of course I would. Even sleeping on the floor of the bedsitter would have been preferable to where I was.

But I had heard those wistful promises too often to believe them any longer. Underneath my mother's bright smiles and his bravado I sensed defeat. Words were easy, and I didn't think they believed that was going to happen, any more than I did.

I just wondered why my mother even bothered moving, when each place she called home was nearly indistinguishable from all the others. Just another dreary room with the cloying smell of boiled vegetables, cheap meat, dust and despair clinging to the walls. Oh, there were attempts to make each place cosy, a bright cushion, a vase filled with wild flowers, a print framed in white, but nothing hid how dismal they were.

The one where I told them what happened to me in Haut de la Garenne was the same as all the others except that it was on the ground floor. They shared the kitchen with the neighbours on the opposite side of the hall, and the bathroom, with its gurgling boiler and shilling slot meter, served the whole household.

I was unaware then of just how difficult it was to rent suitable property. Frank's wages were too low for them to move into anywhere decent. But knowing nothing of their struggle, and being too young to understand it anyway, I was impatient with and disillusioned by their endless empty promises.

That visit, the day I told them what Mr Tilbrook wanted, what he made me do in his office, had started off like all the others, with bright smiles and promises of a lovely day. The bus ride passed the beach I longed to walk on – oh, how I wished it would stop, that my mother and I would alight and spend the day there. I wanted to paddle in the sea, run on the sand, let loose a kite and trail it behind me. I knew that instead I would be sent to play on hard, dusty pavements, while my mother prepared what she called our 'special dinner'.

It would be the same one she cooked every time. Roast chicken, which was carefully divided so that there was enough for Frank and her to eat the following day, potatoes baked in their skins, overcooked vegetables, all generously coated with thick dark gravy. Then, after paying her compliments on how delicious her cooking was, Frank would help clear away, while my mother served custard and tinned peaches. There might not have been much variety, and maybe I did get tired of chicken, but when I compared it to the food at Haut de la Garenne, Frank was right in what he said.

It was after the meal was finished and I was hoping the television would be turned on, that I told my mother and Frank. The telling started not with words but my actions. After refusing Frank's offer of help, my mother had gone to the kitchen, saying, 'No, you stay and talk to Madeleine, see if there's anything on television she might want to watch.'

If only he had done just that – I loved watching anything on the screen.

Then what happened would never have happened.

But it did.

Left alone, he fumbled for something to say while I listened to the domestic sounds of plates being scraped, water being run and my mother humming a tune I didn't recognise. In the clumsy way that men often talk to little girls not their own, he tried to engage me in conversation. To questions such as what I liked at school and what were my favourite programmes on television, he received a blank stare. He resorted to telling me I was a good little girl and would soon be back living with them. 'Madeleine, I want you to think of me as a father,' he said, brushing the top of my head with his thick calloused fingers. 'Now what do you say to that?'

Now I understood what he wanted. I knew what 'good little girl' meant. Just for a moment I went numb, but then fear – fear of seeing his wrath – told me to do what he wanted.

As I had been trained to do, I smiled up at him. Convinced he wanted the same as Mr Tilbrook, I leant against him, then slid my small hand across his stomach until I felt his belt buckle beneath my fingers. It was stiffer than the one Colin Tilbrook wore and my fingers were busy fumbling with it when Frank shouted: 'Hey! What do you think you're doing?' He grabbed my hands and held them by my sides. As I looked up, startled and mystified, I saw that his face had turned a bright red. His expression was a combination of anger and something that looked very much like fear.

'I'm – I'm undoing your belt,' I stuttered.

He pushed me roughly aside. The repugnance on his face made me cringe. I felt heat scorching my face as I wondered what I had done wrong.

'Maureen! Maureen, get in here now!' he shouted to my mum.

And my mother, anxious, rushed in. 'Whatever is the matter, Frank?'

'Your daughter, that's what the matter. Now, Madeleine, tell your mother what it was you just did.'

'I . . .'

'Well, she can't have done much, Frank,' my mother started. Then, seeing that my eyes were welling with tears, she said gently, 'What is it, Madeleine?'

I turned my head away, as I didn't want to see his flushed, shocked face or my mother's worried one. I couldn't find the words to explain what I had done and, knowing they were waiting for me to speak, I was frightened and confused. More than anything I wanted to be held, to be told that everything was going to be all right, that they were not angry with me.

But I was six and unable to put those needs into words. Instead I stared out of the window, as though the view through the panes was the most fascinating I had ever seen. Behind me I could hear their voices, but I stayed still, gazing at lines of washing, a patch of blue sky and next door's orange cat sunning himself. I remembered he was called Marmaduke and that my mother had said it was a silly name.

Outside nothing had changed, but I felt the air behind me growing oppressive as my mother asked Frank again what the matter was.

Then, to my shame, I heard him, his voice tinged with disgust, telling my mother how I had tried to undo his belt and her shocked 'No, surely you must be mistaken, Frank. For God's sake, she's only six.'

'No mistake, Maureen. I know what she did. And, look at her, she does as well. So, I have a question now. Has she learnt that from you, then? Watched you with men? Is that the reason you can't have her living with you?'

'Of course not. Don't be stupid. But maybe she's seen something at the home. There are older children there, you know. And some of them have been put in there because they get into trouble.'

'Is that what happened, Madeleine? Have you seen someone do that? Or did some older girls tell you to do it?'

'No,' I whispered. 'It's what Mr Tilbrook tells me to do when he sends for me.'

My mother's face went blank with what I think was grief. Grief that she had failed her child and this was the outcome. Her arm went round me. 'Oh, Madeleine! Is it really true what you're saying? It's not just a story you've heard from the other girls?'

My reply was to burst into tears. My shoulders heaved, my nose ran and racking sobs shook my body. 'Oh, Madeleine!' I heard her say and, at last, she did what I wanted. Making soothing noises, my mother pulled me onto her knee, wrapped her arms round me and rocked me. Gradually my tears were replaced by hiccups, my face was wiped and, not wanting to move, I leant against her shoulder.

Frank, seeing my distress, became almost incoherent with rage. My mother tried to tell him to wait, that I was still upset but, with his jaw set firm and hard, his eyes like flint, he railed against Colin Tilbrook.

'I'll sort that dirty fucking bastard out, Maureen, see if I don't,' he said, fists clenched. 'He won't be so brave when he faces a man, will he? I'll beat the bloody truth out of him, all right.'

'No, Frank,' my mother yelled. 'Don't be stupid! They won't believe us. They'll take her away from me for good. Accuse us of making up lies and putting evil thoughts in her head. I know those people and you don't.'

'Not when you tell them what's happening up there.'

'You don't know what they're like, Frank. They think of us as dirty scum. Anyhow, you think a little girl would be believed? They'll just say it's our fault, that we made her say it. Then they won't even let me visit, let alone have her back. I've lost my sons, Frank, because I couldn't earn enough to put a decent roof over their heads. I can't lose my daughter as well. They can make sure I never see her again.'

There was such a look of defeat about her as those words tumbled out that Frank quietened. He lit a cigarette, puffed angry bursts of smoke out of his mouth, then turned towards us. 'We'll make a plan. Got to get somewhere where she'll be allowed to live.

'Now, Madeleine,' he said, snapping his fingers just in front of my face. 'I mean it, we'll soon have somewhere. I want you to believe that. And if that dirty pervert comes near you again you just say to him that you're going to tell. Will you do that, Madeleine?'

I nodded, although I knew I would never say anything to Colin Tilbrook. He had ways of punishing little girls. But, sitting on the couch huddled up to my mother, I told them what they wanted to hear.

They promised, again, that they would find somewhere to live that would be approved by the authorities.

'I'll find work again,' my mother said, 'even if it means going back to the farms.' This time her words seemed sincere and, for those brief moments, I felt she was focused on the future, our future. That she was determined we would be a family.

'I'll have you home soon,' she said.

Then it was time for me to leave.

My mother took me, and handed me over to the thin man who called himself Mr Tilbrook's deputy. I watched her walking away, shoulders back, her posture erect. Something about the stiffness of her shoulders, the way she did not look back, told me she was crying.

That evening, Colin Tilbrook sent for me.

Now the policeman's voice cut into my thoughts. 'But you did go home?' he repeated.

'Yes,' I replied. 'But not for long.'

'And that wasn't the state's fault, was it?'

I had no reply to that.

He gathered up his notebook and switched off the recorder.

It was interview over.

I walked, straight-backed, out of the office, my face expressionless, my stomach a hard ball, my pulse sky-rocketing. Were they even going to strip me of my good memories?

'I need a drink,' I said to my son.

CHAPTER FIFTEEN

I was somewhere between six and seven when my mother and Frank told me they had found somewhere to live that was big enough for all of us and that the authorities had agreed I could live with them. They were moving there in just a week's time, my mother had added, with one of her bright smiles. Wasn't that wonderful? It was, I agreed. It had to be the best present I'd ever been given.

All that week thoughts of my new life rattled around my brain. Each night, when the lights were dimmed, instead of fear there was a tingle of excitement in my stomach. It was as if the knowledge that I was leaving had cast a safety blanket around me. Colin Tilbrook didn't send for me and the wardens left me alone. Now I think they didn't want my memories to be too clear, or my bruises too fresh.

I dreamt of what it would be like to live in a house – to be part of a family. I remembered hearing children at the crèche being told what to expect when a mummy and daddy had been found for them. Little faces lost their anxious expressions as their new life was described. They were, Mrs Peacock would tell them, going to a proper home where they would have their own bedroom, and the toy box would be theirs alone.

All those things filled my mind plus one other: I would be safe. Never again would I be taken to Colin Tilbrook's office. Nor, when I went to bed, would I lie there quaking with fear, lest I had a nightmare and my feet were hurt again. No more being dragged out of bed and made to stand shivering in the corridor where shadows frightened me.

Remembering that one child had told me her new mummy was giving her a puppy, I asked if I could have one too. A Labrador like Mrs Peacock's. I would look after it, I said, as I pleaded my case. I'd take it for walks, brush it, and not let it get in the way.

'Not just yet, love,' was my mother's response. But she had not said no so, even though I was disappointed, I clung to that hope. The next thing she told me lifted my spirits. 'Oh, Madeleine,' she said, her forehead creased, 'I nearly forgot to tell you that you'll have to go to a different school.'

No doubt she was expecting protests at my having to leave my friends. She didn't know that since Mandy and Ann had left I'd had none. And I, blaming myself for my classmates' aversion, had never confided in her.

Seeing I wasn't upset, she went on: instead of a thirty-minute walk each way, my new school was just down the road from where I would be living. I felt so happy. There, I would no longer be seen as someone bad enough to have been placed in Haut de la Garenne. I would be just like the rest of the children: a girl living with her mum and dad, for Frank had told me he looked on me as a daughter.

Frances brushed my hair that last day. There was, I thought even then, something sad about her. Over my last few weeks she had changed. Gone was her sparkle and that mischievous grin.

'Does Mr Tilbrook send for you too?' I asked her once.

'No,' she had replied, 'he comes to me.'

I wished she could leave, too, I told her.

'Oh, I will, Madeleine. The moment I'm sixteen I'll be free.' She pulled me close then and I felt her breath against my cheek. 'You're going to be happy in your new life,' she said. 'Put everything that's happened here behind you, Madeleine. Promise me?'

'Yes.'

And then she was gone and I was in the lounge waiting for my mother.

Miraculously, my suitcase with everything I had brought with me had appeared that morning. My pretty dress was now too small but it was my doll I wanted and, picking her up, I was relieved to find her unblemished.

'I thought you told me they'd taken everything,' my mother said.

'They had,' I answered, and saw a flash of something like doubt in her eyes.

'Well, you know how I feel about lies,' she said, 'but we'll not talk about it any more. You have it now.'

I knew then she was wondering if everything I had told her was untrue. Or, at least, that she hoped it was.

CHAPTER SIXTEEN

I had thought no further than that I was going to a proper home so I had asked no questions as to how many rooms there were and what it was like. My imagination had painted a picture of places I had seen in storybooks. A house, standing in a large green garden, a smiling mother at the gate and happy children running towards her.

The reality was very different. The morning my mother came for me we caught a bus to Val Plaisant, and, after a short walk, I saw where I was going to live. It was a small building with an iron roof, standing in the middle of an overgrown garden. A few feet away from the back door there was an outhouse with a dark, chipped door. 'The lavatory,' my mother told me, with a small grimace.

She, too, I realised much later, had dreamt of a pretty brick house with a tiled roof and an inside bathroom.

'It needs painting,' she told me, speaking fast, 'but your dad is going to see to that. He's going to make it look like a proper home. You won't recognise it in a few weeks. You'll see. He's already started on the garden. It was just a mass of weeds a week ago.

He's cut back overgrown bushes, trimmed the hedge and started planting vegetables. Potatoes, well, we'd know how to make them grow, wouldn't we?' she said, laughing. 'Carrots and cabbages as well. So we'll have plenty of good tasty stews. Now let's get you inside.' She opened the door and we stepped straight into the sitting room. It was not the lack of freshly painted walls or the smallness of the place – just two rooms and a tiny kitchen – that made me recoil. It was the smell of ingrained dirt, dust and mildew that clung to the walls. As I would come to know in later years, that was the stink of poverty.

My mother flung open the windows. 'Need some fresh air in here,' she said.

'Where's my bedroom?' I asked, only to receive a wan smile.

'Afraid you'll have to share with us,' she told me, as she led me into a room where a double bed was pressed against one wall, a single one against the other. There was no wardrobe and no space for one. Instead there were some hooks on the back of the door, which, judging by the clothes hanging on them, were already proving inadequate.

I swallowed the little lump of disappointment that had risen in my throat. After all, I was free of Haut de la Garenne, free of Colin Tilbrook, and with two people who wanted me. What did it matter if my new home was different from what I had been expecting?

Seeing the almost apologetic expression on my mother's face, I gave her the biggest smile I could and followed her back into the sitting room.

'I think we both deserve a piece of cake, don't you?' she said. I agreed.

As she bustled around the room, I slid my eyes over it. In the corner there was a squat black stove with a pile of firewood next to it. The furniture consisted of a two-seater settee covered with a floral fabric, a small square table, two upright chairs and, standing on a wooden box, a television.

'The church gave us that,' my mother said. 'It was a sort of "welcome to your new home" present,' she added proudly. 'Now, I know it doesn't seem like much at the moment . . .' Again the promises of how it would change came tumbling out. Not just that it would be painted but that the cracked lino would be replaced with nice carpeting, pretty curtains would hang at the windows and everything would be fresh and clean.

'We wanted to get it all done before we came to get you but . . .' She smiled at me then with such warmth, such joy on her face. 'Oh, Madeleine! I just couldn't bear to be without you for one more minute.'

Her arms went round me and drew me close, as I inhaled her scent, the mixture of cigarettes and face powder. All that mattered was the warm, fuzzy feeling of being loved.

'Now, for a special treat, after we've eaten our supper, you can stay up and watch television with Frank and me. Do you know what's on tonight?'

I shook my head. Watching television was only rarely allowed at Haut de la Garenne. '*The Avengers*,' she said, 'with that lovely Diana Rigg. It's one of my favourite programmes. You'll love it. Oh, Madeleine! It's going to be so much fun, you living here. We'll be a proper family and you'll never be taken from me again.'

That day I believed her.

I believed that this was the beginning of a new life.

And, of course, she did, too.

CHAPTER SEVENTEEN

I woke to the sound of bellowing, loud and full of fear, like animals in distress – animals whose instincts were shrieking of danger. But where were they?

Deep breathing and light snores told me my parents were still asleep, so I pulled myself out of bed and tip-toed into the sitting room. I'd been used to the smell of disinfectant and my nose wrinkled at the sour stench of stale beer and cigarettes.

Living with my mother was not quite as I'd expected. There had been no bedtime story from her before I went to sleep. The crèche had made me think moth-ers did that. Instead, we had watched television, I had sucked sweets that Frank had brought home, and he had opened countless bottles of beer.

By the time my eyes were closing with tiredness, my mother's voice had been slurred, her laugh shrill and her cheeks stained with two bright circles of red. I had wished they would stop drinking. The change in them made me feel uncomfortable. That stuff was making them different. But, still, I had enjoyed sitting, squeezed between them, on the settee, watching the leather-clad heroine overpower evil men twice her size.

Now as I fantasised about being able to do the same things as Emma Peel when I was bigger – kick and overpower men like Colin Tilbrook – I realised I needed a wee. I slid the bolt on the back door and went outside, where the bellowing was louder.

The lavatory, with its black-stained toilet that no amount of bleach could improve, was not somewhere I wanted to stay one second longer than necessary. Holding my breath, I sat on the wooden seat. The moment I'd finished, I opened the door and scurried to the back of the garden.

I was not tall enough to see over the hedge where the sounds were coming from. A rusty metal bucket, which Frank used when he was gardening, was the answer to that problem, I decided. Picking it up, I placed it by the hedge. Standing on tiptoe I peered over and saw a lorry full of cows parked in the yard on the other side. A small ramp had been lowered and they were being herded down it, bellowing.

I heard footsteps, looked round and saw Frank approaching. 'You up already?' he asked, making no move to come closer.

Since the day when I had told him and my mother what had been expected of me at the home, he had kept his distance from me when my mother was not present. I think now it was because he didn't wish to scare me or, worse, make me think he wanted the same thing as Colin Tilbrook.

'Why are they being brought there?' I asked because, as far as I knew, cows belonged in fields, not in that long, low building with its outside metal pens.

Frank paused for a moment, cupped his hands around his lighter, and lit his first fag, as he called it, of the day. He dragged deeply on the cigarette, then said, 'Well, it's a bit of a secret, Madeleine. You see, this is where they are brought to be milked. Not many people know that, which is all to our good.'

'Why?'

'You'll find out a little later,' he replied, tapping his nose and giving me a wink. 'Now, come on in and I'll make us some breakfast.'

It was my mother who explained about the milk and how, if we asked nicely, the farmers were generous in giving us some. What she did not tell me was that the building was the final stop for the cows before they were delivered to the abattoir. That a short time after the last drops of milk had been squeezed out a bolt would be shot into their heads. A fact my mother wisely kept to herself.

Instead, after breakfast, she told me I could make myself useful and go and get some. The window in the bedroom led straight onto the wall that separated us from the yard. All I had to do was stand on a chair with my pail, wriggle out and climb down. I don't know why she suggested that when I could have walked round, but she did. To me, it was more of an adventure to approach the farmers that way.

The first time I came face-to-face with one of them, a weather-beaten man, whose old clothes and cap belied the value of his land, I broke out in giggles. The shock of suddenly having a small child land at his feet had nearly made him drop his pipe.

'Well, what do we have here?' he asked, smiling. 'I do believe she's a pretty little milkmaid. Now, where have you come from?'

I pointed at our house.

When he glanced at our dilapidated single-storey building he didn't need to be told that we were poor. 'Your mother sent you, did she?' he asked, with a grin that showed a gap where several teeth were missing.

He called out to someone in a language I didn't understand, which I came to know as 'Jèrriais', or Jersey French, and a boy came running over. 'I think this little milkmaid wants her bucket filled,' he said. 'Take her over. Oh, and if there's a spare bottle or two, fill them as well, then show her how to get back. Can't climb the wall with your hands full, now, can you?' Chuckling to himself, he walked away.

I was led to where a placid-looking cow was being milked and my pail was taken from me. Creamy liquid, still steaming, was ladled in from the bucket under the cow's teats. Once mine was full to the brim, and an extra bottle had been tucked under my arm, I walked, carefully so not to spill a drop, to the front of the house.

Just before I got there, the temptation to drink some became just too strong to resist. One sip led to another until a third of the bottle was gone.

'Have you been helping yourself, Madeleine?' my mother asked. Looking her straight in the eye, I denied it. 'I think you'd better wash the moustache you seem to have grown on your lips if you want me to believe you,' she said, laughing, as she took the pail from me. 'And in future, Madeleine, don't you be lying to me. "Tell the truth and shame the devil," as my mother always told me,' she added, in a voice that still held echoes of laughter.

Those early days I was with my mother and Frank are full of good memories, which still clutch at my heart. I remember those evenings, the three of us sitting on the settee watching television. The fun of going over the wall to meet the farmers and being praised when I returned home with the brimming pail. Helping Frank in the garden and pulling fat potatoes out of the ground for our supper. Those are the good ones.

Then there are the others.

My mother took me to my new school on my first day. It felt so good that this time she was at my side, not a warden. The week before we had visited charity shops, where she had found me a skirt and blazer, and I felt I looked smart. The tiny, community-centred primary school was next to the huge French Gothic cathedral-like church, with its amazing gargoyles. When my mother had shown me where the school was I had stared at those magnificent stone creatures, pretending they were going to come alive and climb off the wall.

From the gate I could see a small playground and, as I walked in, I felt a rush of elation. This, I told myself, would be different. Nobody knew about Haut de la Garenne, and I was the same as all the other children.

I was wrong. The pupils might not have known that I had been in care, but they sensed something different about me, which turned them into a pack determined to make my life difficult.

Their leader was a skinny little blonde girl, a couple of years older than me. Paula, her name was, and the first time we met in the playground I knew she was trouble. Eyes as hard as boiled sweets raked my clothes and a snigger came out of her mouth.

'Nice blazer,' she said, and I felt that she knew it had come from a charity shop. 'So what's your name, then?'

'Madeleine,' I answered, hoping I was mistaken and that she was trying to be friendly.

'What sort of name is that, then?'

'It's Irish,' I answered.

'My mum says they're a dirty lot, so don't come near me.' She walked off, followed by her gang of giggling sycophants.

Every day she had thought of new taunts. I tried to block out the sound of them and not show that they hurt. 'Sticks and stones can break my bones, but words can never hurt me,' I repeated to myself.

But of course they did.

She saw her inability to reduce me to a quivering mess as a challenge and, after a week, she changed tactics. I noticed her looking in my direction, then muttering to her followers, saw them nodding and giggling and wondered what new insults she had thought of. Then, with her head swivelling from side to side, no doubt keeping watch for teachers, she sprinted towards me. Not to knock me down, as I'd thought, but to pinch me so hard that tears filled my eyes, momentarily blinding me, then splashing onto my cheeks.

'Cry baby, cry baby,' she jibed, practically dancing with joy, as she pointed her finger at me.

After that I tried to avoid her, but she always knew where in the playground I was. Once she was sure the teachers were not looking at her she would run at me, pinch and twist my flesh until I cried. Then the finger would point and the jibes begin.

Each time I saw her coming my mind blurred with fear. And when she mocked me for my weakness, I heard, 'Naughty girl, naughty girl,' in my head, rather than 'Cry baby, cry baby,' and the fear was replaced by anger, which intensified each day.

Revenge was what I wanted. I lay in bed and dreamt of turning the tables. Somehow it would be me making her cry. Me pointing a finger and she feeling afraid. A plan took root, which I decided to put into action.

One morning I hung around near the school gates. I wanted to get her before she met up with her group.

She smirked when she saw me. 'Hiding, are you, little scaredy-cat?' She hissed, with a sneer.

I waited for her to make the first move. I knew that, even without an audience, she wouldn't be able to resist hurting me. I forced myself to look scared and she grinned. Her arm snaked out and her fingers pinched my side. Pain shot through me, but this time I didn't cry. Instead I grasped her arm and sank my teeth into it. She screamed and tried to hit me but, laughing at my success, I ran off.

My elation did not last long. Her shrieks brought a teacher running. Her arm was examined, the tooth marks exclaimed at, and a finger pointed to where I was. The teacher glared at me as she led away my sobbing tormentor.

I was taken to the headmaster's office. I was not asked to explain why I had done such a thing. I could have pulled my jumper up and shown him my bruises. Maybe if he had been a woman I would have done but, faced with the anger that came to me from the opposite side of the desk, I sat mutely. I tried to read the expression on his face but, because his back was in front of the window, I couldn't see it.

My mother was sent for. Words such as 'unacceptable' and 'cannot tolerate such a display of anger' spun round the room, while she, in crumpled clothes, sat apologetically in front of the grey-haired headmaster.

'I am sorry,' she kept repeating, as my sins were listed, 'so sorry,' and I saw a flash of fear in her eyes. 'You're not going to expel her, are you?' she asked, her voice almost cracking with worry.

The headmaster's severe expression was replaced with one of sympathy. 'No, not this time,' he said, less sternly than he had spoken before. 'I know some of the problems she's had . . . well, that you've all had. Perhaps her behaviour stems from being in that home. I know there are a lot of problem children there. And she's still very young. I believe that the best place for a child is with her family. You and I know what could happen if I expelled her, don't we?'

'Yes, I do.'

'Your job, Mrs Ferguson, is to make sure that she understands the consequences if she ever does something like that again.'

My mother thanked him profusely for giving me another chance. He told her that as I was being suspended for a week she would have plenty of time to make sure I understood. 'And there'll be time for things to calm down here,' he said. My mother held my hand tightly as she walked briskly and silently along the corridor and through the doors. It was not until we were outside the gates that she stopped. 'Madeleine, whatever made you do such a thing?' she asked. 'Don't you know how wrong that was?'

'She started it,' I protested. 'She kept pinching me.'

'But she didn't bite you. That's very bad, Madeleine. You must promise me that you'll never do something like that again.'

Of course I did, several times.

But I couldn't understand why Paula's pinching had not caused nearly as much trouble as my biting had. 'It was unfair,' I said to myself mutinously, as tears of frustration stung my eyes, tears that, for once, my mother ignored.

'That, Madeleine,' said Frank, later that evening, 'is not how you deal with bullies. Stand up to them, yes, hit back, but never leave those sort of marks. Promise me that you'll never do it again?'

And I promised again.

I returned to school after my week of being with my mother. She had told me what would happen if I was expelled. 'You'll be taken away again.'

'You will, love,' Frank had confirmed.

How, then, can I stop her if she starts again? was all I thought, feeling miserable at the prospect of returning to school.

I needn't have worried. When I went back, Paula and her friends gave me a wide berth. I think she had been questioned by the headmaster. After all, why would I have attacked a bigger child if not provoked?

My relief was short-lived.

She was replaced by someone worse. Much worse.

This time it was a sullen, dark-haired boy who was both taller and wider than me. The first time I saw him I wanted to walk away from him as fast as I could. I had a feeling that danger was near. When his eyes met mine, they were dark and expressionless.

The same eyes I had seen in Haut de la Garenne.

His name was George and his bullying didn't stop at the playground. Since I wasn't part of a group, I was vulnerable to him. And he had noticed that Frank gave me money when he took me to school. 'Just enough to buy a treat on your way home,' he said, every time he pressed a few coins in my hand.

George followed me when I went to the shops for my parents and hung around near where we lived. The money that was mine he wanted for himself. 'Hello, Madeleine, I'm watching you, girl,' was all he said the first time he spoke, but it was enough to make me afraid.

The next day he followed me from the school until we were out of sight of either teachers or pupils. 'Give it to me,' he said, in flat tones. 'I know you got some money. I saw your dad give it to you.'

'No! It's mine! Leave me alone!' I screamed at him.

Before I could make my legs run as fast as they could, a powerful punch landed in my stomach. I doubled up, gasping for air. 'Now,' he said, 'hand over that money.' I did.

The next day, and the one after, George was outside the school watching me, and when Frank strode off after pressing a few coins into my palm, he was there with his hand out. By the third day I had worked out that he liked hitting me. I had seen too many people, adults and children, in Haut de la Garenne, who took pleasure in inflicting pain on those weaker than themselves, not to recognise the tell-tale gleam in his angry, protruding eyes. Eyes that glittered with suppressed laughter when I handed over the money.

He was aware, after the first day, that I was afraid of him and, having felt the pain of his fist sinking into me, I would have handed over the money if he had just threatened me. But that would have spoilt the fun of watching my face blanch and then, a few seconds later, my gasp for air after the punch.

It was when I realised that he was not going to leave me alone that I talked to my stepfather. I was scared of George, I told him. Could he make it stop? Speak to the boy that I so was afraid of?

'What exactly are you asking me to do, Madeleine?'

'Scare him like he does me?' I answered hopefully.

'What? You expect me to beat up a kid who's not even ten yet? No, that is not going to happen,' he said, ignoring my entreaties for him to do just that. 'Nor am I going to go round and talk to him. I know who you mean. And I agree he's a miserable little sod. Father's in and out of trouble all the time. His mother says she falls down the stairs nearly every week. So he's got a rotten home life, all right. Not that it's any excuse for what he's doing. But no sooner will I have scared off one bully than there'll be another to take his place. No one respects a child who runs to their parents every time they're picked on. You have to learn to fight back.'

'But he's bigger than me.'

'That he is, Madeleine, but being small will make you faster.'

'But . . .' I began, thinking of the trouble I had got into when I had fought back.

As though reading my mind, Frank patted my shoulder and gave me a conspiratorial smile. 'Now, Madeleine, biting is not on. But punching back is all right, as long as you don't start it. He's never going to say that a little kid, and a girl at that, hit him. So, I'm going to teach you how to fight. You have to learn to plant your fist somewhere that hurts. You only get one chance to surprise them.'

In the garden, Frank gave me my first lesson. He made me stand, legs slight apart, and wait for him to throw a punch. 'Now, listen, girl,' he said repeatedly, when I flailed clumsily, 'never have your thumb sticking out. He can take hold of it and twist you to the ground. Tuck it behind your fingers.'

I did.

'Aim here.' He pointed to the part of the body between the ribcage and the stomach.

As he was so much taller than I was, he made a mock body out of some old cushions. 'Imagine that's George,' he said, laughing as my fist sank into the centre of it. 'Attagirl! You got him just right then. That's where you want to hit – knocks the wind out of them quicker than lower down.'

He closed my fist with his large hand. 'Now keep it neat like that, Madeleine,' he instructed. 'And remember what I told you. Speed wins over size. He won't be expecting it. Going to get the shock of his young life, he is.'

Placing my feet where Frank instructed, and using one arm as a guard, I worked at my punches until I could place them just where I wanted.

'Might be better,' said Frank, when he was satisfied with his pupil's progress, 'if you tackle him outside school. Don't want any more problems, do we? Until the weekend, I'm going to take you to school and either I or your mother will pick you up. Until then, you keep practising while he thinks you're just too scared of him to go out on your own.'

That Saturday, half-scared and half-excited, I made my way to the corner shop across from the church. There, for the first time, I was pleased to see George with his habitual smirk and the gleam in his eyes. He swaggered towards me, no doubt thinking of the sweets he was going to buy with my money.

Out came his fists, he drew back his arm and, quick as a flash, I swung under it and hit him. One punch just under his ribs, as Frank had told me, then another for good measure on his chin. With a yell of surprise, he went down.

The look of absolute disbelief, combined with horror, on his face made it all worthwhile. 'Georgie Porgie, pudding and pie,' I chanted, 'isn't going to make the little girls cry.' Then, imitating his swagger, I walked away.

After that, he vanished.

Later I learnt that he had been taken into care. I was not the only child he had stolen from. His father had told him to do it – he used to wait at the bottom of the road to collect the money George took from other children. So I'd been wrong: it hadn't gone on sweets.

When I ever felt sorry for him, I thought of the pleasure on his face when he knew he had hurt me. It might have been his father who had suggested stealing but inflicting pain was George's own idea.

Beating George changed me. I wasn't going to give in to bullies. I practised in the garden and defended myself in the neighbourhood.

CHAPTER EIGHTEEN

2008

The police sent for me again.

This time someone quite different was waiting for me. He was a chunkily built, dark-haired man, wearing a well-cut dark suit, and had warm, deep-set eyes. He shook my hand and thanked me for coming. 'My name,' he said, 'is Graham Power. I asked to meet you today.'

My mouth went dry. Graham Power. Of course I knew who he was. The chief of police. Why did he want to see me?

'How are you bearing up, Madeleine?' he asked, with genuine concern on his face.

'I'm fine,' I replied, although that was untrue. I was not fine at all. My hands were damp with perspiration, my head ached and the butterflies were back in my stomach. I hoped he couldn't smell last night's alcohol on my breath.

If he could, it didn't show on his face. He simply offered me tea, then asked the young policewoman if she would arrange it. 'Oh, and ask for some biscuits, too,' he added, before turning back to me.

He had heard the many complaints, he told me, had read the reports compiled from the interviews, and now wanted to talk to the people concerned.

'Do you believe us, then?' I asked, with a lump in my throat at the thought that I was finally speaking to someone who did.

'Yes,' he replied, 'I do, and I'm not the only one.' As he spoke, I saw in him sadness that such things could have happened to so many children; children who had grown into broken adults.

'Madeleine,' he said, 'I'm sure that this investigation is taking its toll. And I worry that what we're asking of all of you must sometimes be unbearable. Things that you never wanted to think about again, far less talk about, are being dragged out into the open. Do you think you can cope with it for a little while longer?'

'Yes. I can.' I was determined that nothing would sway me from helping us all get justice, I told him. I did not admit that the investigation had invaded my brain and eaten away any thoughts of everything that should be even more important: my marriage and my family. A picture of my daughter's hurt face, and my husband's disappointed one when they had come across me with a tumbler of wine flashed before me and I felt a sharp twinge of guilt. I pushed it aside. 'But,' I added, summoning my courage to say what he might take as criticism, 'there are times when I get despondent. So little seems to have happened.'

'It's an ongoing case, Madeleine. And I'm not going to let up on it. The whole world will be watching Jersey soon. The investigation into Haut de la Garenne is about to break in the news.'

'Does that mean some of the perpetrators will be punished?'

'Yes, it does.'

'But it won't bring back our childhoods, will it?'

Again I saw sadness cross his face; sadness at making me relive a past that, for so many years, I had put behind me.

He had a file in front of him and, opening it, he ran over some of my early life. 'Tell me, Madeleine, how it was that you were sent back to Haut de la Garenne? Was it something you had done? Had you become too difficult at the tender age of seven?'

'I don't think so,' I answered, though a smile played on my lips when I thought of the tough little character I had been.

'But you were taken away from your mother and stepfather and sent back to Haut de la Garenne. Why was that?'

'My mother was ill with glandular fever.' Faltering, I started to explain what that last year had been like, believing that I was talking to someone in authority who cared. And as I talked, the memories of things I'd forgotten about resurfaced. The things that were not part of my happy memories.

It had been hot that summer, flies hovering over food and buzzing around my head. I hated the fat bluebottles. The persistent buzzing, their hairy little legs and those red eyes searching for any crumb they could find to squat on. We covered milk and food, batted them away with rolled-up newspapers, and hung sticky brown fly-paper from the lights. Every day it was splattered with the corpses of tiny winged creatures, but not, I noticed, with one bluebottle.

'It's the cows in the yard over there that bring them in,' my mother said, as though her explanation made them more bearable.

I didn't care why they were in our home. I just knew that I detested them. I had learnt at school that they laid their eggs on dung and fed off it. The thought of their filthy feet walking on anything that was going into my mouth made my stomach turn. I had only to see one descend on the table to become hysterical.

Before the unbearable heat that had turned my home into a furnace came, I had looked forward to the summer holidays. On the day we broke up, I listened for the bell announcing we could leave. As soon as I heard it, I gathered up my school books, rammed them into my satchel and left as fast as I decently could. Goodbyes were called out, then I was outside, rushing towards home.

Six weeks of doing nothing. Six weeks of not agonising over the fact that I still couldn't read. That the letters danced in front of my eyes, impossible to catch. They had sent me for tests. Maybe it was my eyesight, but I knew it wasn't.

'Can you see the letters?' the optician had asked.

I could, but even then I couldn't say what all of them were. I just didn't know. But I had been right: there was nothing wrong with my vision. Now I remembered my embarrassment at being told that.

Graham Power raised his hand to stop my flow of words. 'They never thought to see if you were dyslexic, did they?'

'No. That was never talked about then. They just thought I had difficulty learning. That I didn't concentrate and was too lazy to do my homework. Of course, the teachers became impatient and the children in the class pulled faces and giggled each time I got a word wrong. I mean, we were given homework – we were supposed to learn spellings every night but I could never get them right. They simply didn't believe that I had tried.'

Once again I saw my seven-year-old self in her charity-shop clothes, her cheeks burning with shame at her inability to keep up with the class.

I wasn't to know that when the bell rang for the final time before the holiday it was announcing the last summer holiday in which I believed I was secure.

'We'll go to the beach,' my mother had promised. 'Act like tourists, sit on our towels, make sandcastles and eat ice cream.' Her bright smile flashed as she described her plans for the summer. 'I'll take you to the castle as well, show you more of our island. After all, this is your home. This is where you'll grow up. Now, what do you want to see first?'

'Elizabeth Castle,' I answered, thinking of the stories my teacher had told us of beautiful princesses being rescued by handsome princes. 'Will we see the Queen?' I asked.

'No, Madeleine,' replied my mother, laughing. 'No one lives there any longer.' Seeing my face drop, she added, 'But there is an ice-cream shop nearby.'

She kept her promise. The day after my holiday began we packed some sandwiches to eat on the beach and walked across to Elizabeth Castle. Scrambling over rocks and sand, simply enjoying the warmth of the sun, the sound of the sea and being with each other. As my mother had promised, there was a small kiosk with pictures of the ice-creams sold there. The sun promptly melted the two scoops of chocolate piled into a cone, making it run over my hands and dribble down my chin.

My mother laughed and dabbed it off. 'Better eat it quicker,' she said, taking a lick of hers.

We carried on walking along the front until we reached St Aubin. Stopping to lean against the sea wall, she pointed to the little white egrets with their long black legs and slender black beaks wading in the shallows. When we reached the giant stepped sea defences, we sat, watching the speed of the incoming tide and eating our sandwiches.

She was happy that day. We both were. I felt so close to her. The sun had turned her face and shoulders a pale gold and, with the sea breeze blowing her hair, she looked young and carefree. That is the picture I try to keep shiny-bright in my mind – her standing on the rocks, eyes sparkling, hair loose, laughing at something I had said.

How she was before it all went wrong again.

'You loved your mother very much,' Graham Power said gravely.

'Yes, I did. I loved both of them.'

I don't remember how long it was after that day that my mother became ill. Less than a week, I think. I could hear her in the morning, vomiting into the bucket placed by her bed. I looked after her because Frank had to leave early each morning for work. Each day she seemed to grow weaker. Her face glistened with sweat and her hair clung damply to her neck. Dark shadows formed around her eyes and I seldom saw her bright smile.

I wrung out cloths in cold water and placed them on the back of her neck. Brought cool drinks to where she lay limply, either on the settee or in bed. All I was able to do when it came to feeding us was to pour milk over cereal and butter slices of white bread.

Every day it grew hotter and she more tired.

We had to open windows and doors and, through them, came the flies, followed by mosquitoes. I had itchy lumps all over my body. I longed to go back to the beach, have my hair ruffled by the breeze, and cool my feet in the water. But, after that first day, she was never well enough.

Her face lost colour and became wrinkled while her figure thickened.

The holidays ended at the same time as the heat left the sun. It was then I learnt why she was so tired and why Frank looked worried. She tried to sound bright when she told me that by Christmas I was going to have a baby brother or sister. 'Won't that be lovely, Madeleine?' she said.

I didn't think so.

With the departure of summer, draughts crept under doors, windows ran with condensation, and then, instead of being hot, we were cold. The roof leaked at night and I could hear water dripping into buckets. The small black stove gave out a thick, pungent heat that didn't penetrate our bedroom. And, oh, how I hated going to that outside lavatory in my nightclothes.

It was nearly Christmas when my baby brother arrived. A tiny, red-faced scrap, who cried loudly. My mother was too weak to feed him, and at night it was Frank who heated the bottles and gave them to him.

The nurse came, her sharp eyes glancing round the room at the bucket filled with nappies, and at my mother's wan face. 'You have to see the doctor,' she said firmly.

He arrived the next morning and his diagnosis was that my mother had glandular fever. 'You need to eat fresh eggs, plenty of fruit and green vegetables. Drink lots of fresh milk. Good nourishing food, that's what you need.' From the expression on his face when he looked around our home, he had little faith in it happening.

The welfare people knocked on our door within days of his visit. I don't know what was said, only what the outcome was. It was my mother who told me, her face a twist of anguish, that I was being returned to Haut de la Garenne. 'Just for a few weeks until I'm better,' she said, but the words had a hollow ring. The last of her confidence had been ripped away by her illness and I sensed that she did not believe in the 'few weeks' story.

At this point Graham Power asked, 'And was she offered no help?'

'None,' I replied, 'and Frank worked so hard and earned so little.'

I remembered my mother's bitterness when she told me why we were so poor. 'Because he's not a Jersey man, the bosses don't pay him fairly. They look down on us. "Poor white trash", that's what they call us. But we're all right to work for them.'

'But you weren't returned to your mother when she recovered. It was much longer than that. You stayed in Haut de la Garenne for more than a year before you joined her again. And it doesn't take that long to recover from glandular fever, does it?'

'No. The place she lived in was not suitable for two children. They accepted the baby sharing their room, but not me.'

'And she didn't protest, knowing how unhappy you'd been there?'

Thinking of the fleeting expression of doubt I had seen on my mother's face when my suitcase was returned, I said, 'Children aren't always believed, are they? I mean later on, how often did we try to tell adults? We even told the police, you must know that, but we were just laughed at.'

I remembered the social worker who had made the decision that I was to be returned. I begged not to be sent back there. 'Your mother isn't well enough to look after you,' was her only response.

With tears coursing down my face, I promised I'd help her look after my baby brother. I wanted to stay with my family, I told her, but she didn't listen.

'As soon as your mother is a little better she'll come and visit you there,' she said, trying to placate me. 'She'll take you out at weekends.'

'But when can I come home?'

She didn't answer.

'I'll come and see you,' my mother kept saying. 'You won't have to stay there long.'

'Promise?'

'I promise.'

It had been, as Graham Power reminded me, more than a year.

'When she asked for me to be returned, the authorities just said that the house wasn't suitable. And did they really believe that Haut de la Garenne was?' I asked sadly.

'Well, it's become clear that it wasn't,' he replied.

CHAPTER NINETEEN

I watched Graham Power's expression change subtly. A tightening of the jaw, a slight frown. Now, I realised, he wanted to ask me more questions, which would be painful. I understood that, up to now, everything he had persuaded me to talk about had been a preamble. He had wanted to put me at my ease and he had.

Something about him made me trust him. He had our welfare at heart, of that I was convinced.

'Tell me what it was like for you when you went back, Madeleine. You were that much older, more aware of what was taking place in the home. In one of your statements you told the police officers that Colin Tilbrook continued to assault not just you but also other children, and that certain members of the staff did so as well. And not only that, there were visitors to the home. Men who came for one purpose only. One of them, you say, was a well-known celebrity and another, who has already been convicted for his crimes, acted as Father Christmas. You said, too, that beneath the home there was a maze of rooms where orgies took place. Is that correct?'

'Yes.'

And I forced my mind back to that time.

As that carousel of images and emotions spun in my head, so the words of what happened spilt out.

When I had crossed the threshold of the home on my return, my body had shaken. I watched my mother walk away until the sea mist's shadows swallowed her. I wanted her to look back, run to me and give me one last hug, but I knew she wouldn't, for I would have seen her tears.

A hand fell on my shoulder. One with black hairs sprouting on the fingers, reminding me of a spider. 'Welcome home, Madeleine,' he said.

This time I knew what lay in store for me in that dark, silent place. I had never experienced terror before. Fear, yes, stomach-clenching fear, but not terror. There was no rational thought in my head, just instinct, and that instinct was telling me to run. But my body did not respond. I was frozen to the spot. Through the fog of my fear I knew that there was no place to run to.

The hand lifted and the man gave me a tight smile, one that both mocked and frightened me, then told a warden to take me to the dormitory. The only person I wanted to see was Frances and there I stood, by the bed she had slept in.

'She's not here any longer,' said the warden, who had escorted me.

'But she isn't sixteen yet,' I blurted out. Frances had told me there was no chance that she would be allowed to leave before then.

'She's been sent away. Got herself in trouble. But she'll be back, never worry.'

But I did worry. Without her I felt I had no protection.

I was sure that Colin Tilbrook would send for me that night; that a boy would walk into the lounge and say I was wanted.

But I was wrong, it was not him who sent for me.

There were others, I was to learn, who shared his interests.

They came for me while I was drifting off to sleep, two female wardens, with the sour stench of alcohol on their breath. 'Out you get,' they said, pulling the sheets off me.

Surely they're not going to make me stand in the corridor on my first night, I thought. I felt the urge to pee and a tiny trickle leaked out. 'Please don't let them see it,' I prayed.

'How old are you now, Madeleine?' one asked

'Seven, miss.'

'I see your stay with your family hasn't made you forget your manners,' said the other, then broke out in giggles. 'Oh, don't be scared! We're not going to punish you. You haven't done anything wrong, have you?'

'No, miss.' A tiny bit of confidence came to me. I knew they had been drinking and were in a good humour, so whatever they wanted with me wasn't going to be bad, was it?

It was.

They took me to a room and all I can remember of it was that it had high, arched windows. 'Now,' said the younger of the two, 'let's get Madeleine something to drink. Make her feel as good as we do.'

A glass was handed to me and my fingers wrapped round it.

'Say cheers, Madeleine,' they chorused, as they lifted their glasses and swallowed the contents.

'In one, dear.' A finger went under the glass and pushed it up to my mouth. A face loomed near mine, so close I could see the pores in her flushed cheeks. 'I expect you like playing games, Madeleine. Doctors and nurses, perhaps?'

'You show me yours if I show you mine,' said her friend and, as she spoke, the room tilted and my legs turned to jelly.

Arms held me, then pushed me down on a couch. A wet mouth covered mine, sticky and rubbery, and I tried vainly to turn my head away. Then her friend ran her hands down my body. 'A nice little chicken, all right,' she said.

My nightdress was lifted. Sharp-nailed fingers touched me between my legs. My head was pulled to their breasts, clothes slithered off and my hands were forced to stroke their bodies. Another drink was given. And, as the last drop was swallowed, the time there drifted away.

My head was dragged down again, my lips forced to touch places that I didn't want to touch. All the time I fought nausea. 'We'd better get her back to the dormitory,' I heard a voice say, through the mist.

And, at last, my ordeal was over.

I was half carried, half dragged along those dark corridors by the two wardens, who were still giggling at my efforts to walk. I don't know how long they had kept me in that room. I remember that I was dazed, confused and frightened.

In the morning I couldn't open my eyes – the lids seemed to be stuck together. My mouth was dry, and my head ached so much it was as though it was splitting in two.

Had that evening happened? Had I been taken out of bed? Had female hands done those acts? Or was it another of my nightmares? An endless blur of pictures, all bad, spun in my head.

But I knew that it had all been real.

MADELEINE VIBERT

At school all I wanted to do was sleep. I was so tired that I felt my eyes closing, which the teacher took to be another sign of my lack of interest in lessons, and voiced her recriminations loudly. No matter how angry she became, it made no difference. The letters made even less sense, and simple arithmetic was beyond me. When I looked at her I could see her mouth moving but the sounds stopped forming words.

Maybe if I had lived at home she might have asked if I'd had a late night, been allowed to watch too much television, perhaps. Questions I had heard her ask other children. It was unlikely, though, that it entered her head that I might have been deprived of sleep. After all, I lived in a children's home, where we were strictly supervised. And if she had asked me, would I have been believed if I had talked?

There were many nights when sleep was denied us. Children in the home aped the adults' tyrannical behaviour. Some teenage boys forced sex on girls, and others on younger boys. Some girls assaulted younger ones. It was long after the night when the wardens had taken me to the room with arched windows that I was woken by a girl who had crawled into bed with me. 'I saw you go with them,' she said as, pushing her nightdress up, she climbed on top of me. In a parody of the sex act she bounced up and down on my smaller body, her face pressed against mine, making it impossible for me to cry out. But, in any case, I was too frightened to scream. What good would it have done me?

The wardens must have been aware of what went on. They had little listening devices fixed to the walls that told them of any talking. This was clearly not something they had any interest in putting a stop to. The wardens who would come into the room might be the same ones who had corrupted the ten-year-old girl who was abusing me. After she left me, I lay there, paralysed.

Was there no safe place left? No one I could trust?

At that age I didn't understand everything that was happening. I knew it was wrong, but I didn't know why. Only that it made me feel unclean.

A few days later the girl came up to me and offered me some sweets. I wanted to knock them out of her hand, to hit her as I had hit the school bullies. But her face wore an expression that I can only describe as hopeful. She hoped I would be her friend. I dipped my fingers into the bag, pulled out a toffee and popped it into my mouth. We were just two children making a tentative effort to be normal. One was already an abuser, the other her victim.

'What happened to her, do you know?' Graham Power asked.

'She ended up working at the home. Left for a short time and suddenly she was back. There was no sign then of the girl who had tried to befriend me with sweets. She wasn't the only one, either. There was a boy who had been brutalised – I gave the police his name. And he, in turn, abused children as soon as he had a bit of authority. So the cycle just kept repeating itself.'

I went on to talk about Colin Tilbrook. He was dead, but lived on in my nightmares. 'He took his pick of the girls,' I told Graham Power. 'Chose which one he was going to favour that night.'

'Can you clarify for me what you remember? How you knew what was going on with the other children?'

For a few seconds, I squeezed my eyes shut, conjuring up the image of that black-clad figure creeping into the dormitories. Whatever I had thought the screams and cries meant when I was five, at seven I knew what was happening. I might have been in bed, might even have fallen asleep, but I think there is something in us that sends a message saying, *Danger*. Even when we're asleep we receive it.

I would wake up knowing something was wrong. Keeping my breathing as even as I could, I would strain my eyes to see. And there he would be, that darkly clothed figure, holding a pillow.

One of the policemen, who had interviewed me previously, had asked whether it might have been a nightmare.

It was not.

Neither was it a figment of my imagination.

I saw him looking down at girls who, like me, pretended to be asleep. Of course, he knew which one he wanted but he enjoyed the game of putting fear into us. He took pleasure in watching little girls pretending they were unaware of him, as they prayed for him to pass them for someone else.

'And to what use was the pillow put?'

That question took me back to when I was a frightened seven-year-old, my stomach clenched, my hands damp, as, through half-closed eyes, I watched him. Watched his hand, which had run over my body so often, pull back the bedclothes before he slid into a child's narrow bed. Then a girl trying to get away, her limbs thrashing, his hands pushing her back, her mouth opening to scream, and the pillow pressing down on her pleading face.

I had watched those pointless struggles, seen his head bending close to her ear, but although I couldn't hear what was said, it wasn't long before I learnt what he whispered: unless she kept still he would hold that pillow over her face until she turned blue. And should she think that the moment he released it she could scream, well, he would put it back again. For longer. Did she understand?

She did and, hearing those words, lay still. Not another murmur of protest or muffled cry left her. The only sound we heard was his thrashing, his grunts, until the loudest one told us he had finished. Then, when he left her, she let small choking, mewing sobs escape her.

All of that I told Graham Power as briefly as I could.

I didn't tell him that I'd had no need to search deeply among my forty-year-old memories to bring out that picture. I had only to think of the nightmare that haunts me. The shadowy figure still drifts through it. And, as I wake, he is still there in the shadows and the sounds of little girls' sobs are in my ears.

'Fear is how we were governed and how we were controlled,' I told Graham Power, as I described, as best I could, just how we were infused with it.

It had started with the warden's bed inspection. Those women's noses would almost quiver as they detected the faint whiff of urine where a terrified child had wet herself. Sheets were pulled off, curses uttered, and a small figure, with tears shining on her jaw and at the corners of her mouth, would gather up her bedding and stagger to the laundry.

There were a thousand means of taking away our dignity. We were made to wait for our food until the numbers of our section were called. Silence was inflicted upon us. Our few personal possessions were taken. Food was withheld as a punishment, and visitors were sent away. To name just a few.

That day, I told Graham Power what had happened in the home. The times I had run away. The detention rooms. The men who came. The boys who were taken out to the bunker. And, last, I told him about the swimming-pool.

There were other things I could have told him, but I didn't have time. I didn't know when I left that that was the only time I would talk to him. Neither he nor I were aware of the events conspiring against him and us.

CHAPTER TWENTY

That night, after I'd talked to Graham Power, I sat deep in thought and painful memories. The smug, hard faces of the wardens swam in front of me. Oh, how I hoped there would be retribution for their crimes. Then, perhaps, we could find some peace.

My mind slipped back to the time I had spent with my mother and Frank. If only I had remained with them, how different my life would have been. My mother had been rehoused. This place, she was told, was suitable for children. I didn't know what instruction the authorities gave her then, but I'm sure it was that she should look after herself and her two children. That for me to be allowed to remain with her she must keep her home clean, cook nourishing meals and cut down on smoking and drinking, especially the latter.

The day I walked away from Haut de la Garenne again, I had no idea that my mother's actions would be scrutinised. I only knew that I was escaping.

'I'll never come back here,' I said to myself as, once again, I picked up my suitcase and, with my mother, walked away from the bleak, grey building.

Our new home was on what is known in Jersey as a housing estate and, in Britain, a council one: rows of grey houses, surrounded by broken bicycles, discarded prams and beaten-up old cars, rather than neat hedges and leafy trees. The flat, deemed suitable for children, was in 'the alcoholic block', as Le Geyt Flats was nicknamed.

At the beginning I was just happy to be back with my family and, an extra bonus, that I was to attend the same school as I had before. It was just round the corner from where we were living. I didn't think that the children would have forgotten me after a year. And I had left with a reputation for being handy with my fists, which would, I hoped, ensure that I wasn't bullied again.

It took a few weeks for the euphoria to fade.

My mother had changed. A life of unfulfilled dreams had taken their toll. She had finally reached the age when, instead of dreaming of a bright future, she looked back on her sad memories. Her wide smile had disappeared, as had her promises of a better life. When I came home from school there was no smell of cooking, and the flat didn't look as though she'd cleaned it. There was seldom any pretence that it was just a weekend celebration, when she picked up the bottle. The swallowing of its contents was a joyless drowning of reality.

First, there was a gasp of satisfaction as the first glug slipped down her throat, then bursts of laughter that quickly became shrill. I would hear another bottle being opened and, with a knot in my stomach, wait for what must follow. Recriminations, tears, the unsteady walk to bed, shouts and curses, then deep snores.

In the year I had been away, Frank, who had earlier opened bottles of beer good-naturedly and brought me fizzy drinks, had lost his energy and aged. With one wage coming in and a penchant for both alcohol and cigarettes, something had had to give: food and heating. In the tin-roofed house, we had been either too hot or too cold, but it had had a garden, which had provided us with steady crops of vegetables. To make matters worse, the barns where the cows had been milked had been moved so I could no longer collect milk for us.

Even in those shabby bedsitters my mother had taken care to keep the places clean. Maybe it was the realisation that this was where she had ended up that had wiped out the last of her optimism. Nappies were piled in the bucket, my little brother's face was forever grimy and the aroma of casseroles and roast chicken was mainly absent.

People knocked on the door to see if they could borrow money or a cigarette – 'I'm desperate for a fag,' I would hear a voice slur.

I overheard Frank saying to my mother that maybe they'd better be more careful. 'Don't want those do-gooders knocking on the door and finding you still in bed, do we?' he said.

That weekend, with Frank's help, there was a flurry of activity. Floors were mopped, windows cleaned, washing done and food cooked. Makeup was once more on my mother's face and the drink was limited to just a couple of beers.

'I like a drink,' my mother told me, as though this was a secret to which I was finally privy, 'but I don't want to end up like those other women, do I?' She was referring to a couple who could be heard carousing from one end of the street to the other, as they made their unsteady way home from the pub.

For a week after that, things seemed to have returned to normal. Frank's cheerful whistle could be heard once more. The kitchen smelt fragrant, my little brother was clean, the social workers had been, then left with satisfied smiles, and my mother had not been drinking too much.

It was just when I thought our lives had taken a turn for the better that my uncle Eugene came to stay and everything changed again. He arrived when we were sitting together, watching television. A knock at the door and a blurry voice announced his arrival. In he staggered, a bottle in one hand and a bag of fish and chips in the other. A big, blustery man, thick in the chest, muscled in the arms, with a drunk's insincere smile and bloodshot eyes. Needed somewhere to stay for just a few days, he said.

He could sleep in the baby's room. My mother and Frank would take him in with them. It was only a small single bed in a room not much bigger than a cupboard, but it would have to do.

That was the first time, and when Uncle Eugene left, Frank found his war medals had been stolen. He came back a few weeks later. I had watched him approaching the flat from my window and seen the wide-legged gait that told me he was already intoxicated. Again, a bottle of whisky was produced, glasses raised and I was sent to bed. This time, instead of lying in bed listening to their voices growing slurred, I heard Frank getting angry and Uncle Eugene shouting that he had been insulted. He was no thief! How dare Frank say he was? I heard my mother trying to calm them both down.

I crept out of bed and, through my door, saw both men lurch to their feet. A fleshy fist sank into Frank's stomach before he had time to put up his fists. My mother screamed, furniture was smashed and the baby howled in fright.

Anywhere else the police would have been called, but the people in the alcoholics' flats had their own issues with them.

He only stayed once more. That 'once more' brought my nightmares back.

As I woke, I smelt his breath, felt his hand on my shoulder and heard him start to unbuckle his belt. Opening my eyes, I saw, against my wall, a huge black shadow leaning over me. My mouth opened and I screamed. Frank came running. He was holding something – a large piece of wood.

'Out!' he yelled. 'Get out now! Or I swear you won't be able to walk out.' The wood was raised above his head.

Eugene blustered, said he'd stumbled into my room by mistake, thought it was the bathroom.

Frank's face darkened. 'Out of my house, you filthy bit of scum.'

'Don't think you want the police coming round here,' Eugene said. 'I shouldn't think you want to end up in prison. She'd be back in that home so fast her feet wouldn't touch the ground. And we all know what goes on in that place, don't we?' he added, with a sneer. 'Oh, don't you fuss yourself. I'm leaving.' He stumbled to the door and, as he opened it, issued his parting shot: 'Nothing wrong with a bit of firm flesh, Frank. S'pect you've been fiddling her yourself.' With that, he was gone.

And now the outside world no longer felt safe.

CHAPTER TWENTY-ONE

It didn't take my mother long to start drinking again. Frank tried to curtail the amount, but he was at a loss as to what to do. Food became scarce again. It seemed that what Frank earned wasn't enough to feed us and pay for the bottles of gin my mother now craved. At school, as I qualified for free lunches, I was able to stave off hunger by asking for seconds. And when the bottles of milk were handed out, I tried to smuggle mine back to the flat.

At weekends the golden sands of West Park beach provided me with a means of making some money. Careless holiday-makers left behind their empty lemonade bottles. I would stuff as many as I could carry into a bag and take them to the nearest café for the refunds. With the money I made, I would treat myself to a portion of newspaper-wrapped chips. There were even times when I found enough to go to Funland with my friends and play on the slot machines. At home, questions were seldom asked as to where I had been, as both my mother and Frank had their own problems.

My mother had sunk back into a depression that only gin relieved and then just for a short time. I would help as much as I could, by washing my baby brother's nappies and hanging them out, cleaning and washing-up. But it was never enough.

Weekends were the worst: without school dinners and milk, my stomach rumbled with hunger. As summer faded and winter drew in, there were no more empty lemonade bottles littering the beach, which meant no more hot chips. Of course, there were days when my mother pulled herself together and a thick Irish stew, with more potatoes than meat, was placed on the table. On some Sundays a roast chicken would appear. And on Fridays, if there was extra money in his pay packet from overtime, Frank would come home with bags of vinegar-smelling fish and chips. But there were other days when there was little except stale bread and tinned baby food. It was on one of those days when, feeling hollow with hunger, I went into the church.

I don't know what made me do it, but it was fortunate that I did. I was nibbling one of the small candles in front of the statue of the Virgin Mary when a priest appeared. A grey-haired man with thick, dark-framed glasses, he introduced himself as Father Paul and asked me what I was doing. To which, with the heat rising in my face, I gave him the blankest look I could. I was only too aware that he had caught me stealing.

'Are you so hungry?' he asked gently.

I whispered, 'Yes.' Though all I was thinking then was that I had committed a mortal sin, not just in taking what was not mine but in stealing from the church.

'Come with me,' was all he said. Placing his hand on my shoulder, he led me to the presbytery. He showed me into a book-lined room where winter sunlight gleamed on polished wood. 'Wait here. I just have to go through to the kitchen to see if I can find you something a bit tastier than those candles.' A mischievous smile lit his face, making it almost boyish.

I gazed round nervously and wondered what was going to happen. I didn't have long to wait. 'Sorry it's all cold,' he said, placing a plate of French bread, cheese and pickles in front of me. 'Tuck into that and then we can talk. You can tell me why you are so hungry, and then I'll take you home.'

I told him, between mouthfuls, of how my mother was struggling. That there was never enough food in the house and, sometimes, no heating. And, yes, I also admitted that she drank. I knew it was disloyal but the words just slid out.

'People find solace in different ways,' he said kindly, 'and it's not my place to pass judgement.'

Once I had finished talking and eating my eyelids began to droop with tiredness. 'I think I'd better drive you back,' he said. Drowsily I followed him outside to where a sparkling clean cream Morris Minor was parked. 'In you get,' he said, opening the door. One of those new seatbelts was strapped round me. 'Keeps you safe,' he told me, with a smile, when I asked what it was for. Once he had climbed into the driver's seat he asked me to repeat my address, then drove sedately to our flat.

Once my mother had recovered from the shock of seeing me return with a priest in tow, tea was offered. He accepted, seated himself and waved aside her flurry of apologies at the house being untidy and the absence of biscuits. He told her he knew it was hard for some families, especially the Irish ones. That one income was never enough, and was there anything he could do? 'You have only to ask. That is what the Church is here for,' he told her, when tears flooded her eyes. Before he left he assured her that he would arrange for extra blankets to be delivered, as well as a box of groceries and two sacks of coal. A few weeks later he brought round a huge hamper. 'For Christmas,' he told us, then invited me to the children's party.

As well as that party, with its huge tree, a present for every child, there are other good memories. There were times when I was nothing other than a carefree child. Playing on the beach with my friends, sneaking into the Hôtel Le Coin, where we pretended we belonged to holiday-makers' families. Making friends with their children and, when I said my mother was resting with a headache, being given ice-cream by someone's mother.

The day of the accident I came out giggling from the hotel that, once again, I had got away with whatever I'd been doing. I was so pleased with myself that I paid no attention as to where I was walking. I heard my friend scream out my name and looked up to see a coach full of tourists bearing down in my direction. Then the world went black.

I woke up in Intensive Care with my mum staring at me. I learnt later that I had a broken collarbone, a very bruised body and concussion. On seeing my eyes flicker open, my mother stretched out her hand and took mine. Her mouth quivered as she tried to smile. 'Oh, thank God you're all right, Madeleine,' she said, and squeezed my fingers. My eyes closed again. Trying to stay awake was just too much of an effort. I heard her voice as though from far away: 'What were you doing? You could have been killed!' she was saying. 'I've been worried out of my mind. You're never to go back to that hotel again, do you hear? Never again!'

Then, mercifully, I slipped back into sleep.

The coach driver came to visit, bringing chocolates and flowers. He was so sorry, he kept repeating. I had just stepped out in front of him.

Then another visitor came.

She was from the authorities. 'It's not working, you being at home,' she said. 'Your mother cannot control you.'

I was allowed home for the remainder of the holidays.

When they ended I went back to Haut de la Garenne. The social worker took me there.

I had already said goodbye to my mother.

'I'll visit,' she said, avoiding my eyes.

I noticed that this time she made no promise that I would be there for just a short time. We both knew I would not.

I was older now, more able to fight back, I thought, all the time feeling sick with dread. Nothing could be worse than being returned to Haut de la Garenne, which I'd thought I had left behind – which I had survived, my inner voice added. Ever since I had been told of my fate I had tried to convince myself that I would be all right.

I didn't manage to.

And I was right. It was going to get worse.

The Jordans were due to arrive.

CHAPTER TWENTY-TWO

2008

Another phone call, another interview. This time I wasn't worried for I was sure it was Graham Power I was going to meet.

It was not.

The first policeman was there, in his dark suit and crisp white shirt, with the obligatory policewoman seated next to him. There were few preliminary questions. Instead he picked up a file, opened it and looked intently at me. 'Madeleine, in the statement you gave Graham Power you said there was a swimming-pool. That it was in the basement.'

'There was one in the basement.'

'The basement, you say? Your statement makes it sound as though there was a maze of secret rooms under the floors. But really, Madeleine, the space down there is just that, a void. It's only four foot high. There are no signs of a pool. No evidence that it was ever there.'

He paused, glanced down at his notes, while I remained silent.

'However, there is one that, no doubt, you swam in. One that was donated to the home by a kind benefactor. It's outside, not hidden away. But there is nothing, absolutely nothing, to indicate that there was ever a pool somewhere beneath the ground. There isn't the space for it in those voids you refer to as cellar rooms. Is it possible that your memories are a little confused?'

Now, I know that my memory can be a little fuzzy. And it was the experience of a very young child that I was trying to recall. I accept that sometimes I'm not sure if it's a nightmare I remember or a fact. I wonder, though, if some of the things I have put down to bad dreams are really memories that visit my subconscious when I'm in the half-waking state that daybreak brings. But some are just too clear, too sharply etched into my brain, to be anything but the truth.

Traumas, I have been told, are often wiped out of our conscious memory. Maybe that is why some of the interviewees found giving evidence so difficult. If so, I wondered, why had that not happened to my recollections of childhood? I can recall words, although the faces of those speaking and their voices are less clear.

'It was there then,' I said. 'I'm not saying it was as large as the one outside. Of course it wasn't. It was more the size of what we would now call a plunge pool. But then, to a child, it seemed big – big and frightening.'

'So tell us, Madeleine,' the policewoman said, 'what use was made of a pool we have no record of ever being there?'

'It was where the men had parties.'

'How many men?'

'Sometimes as many as ten. They would be there when we arrived.'

And through those dusty corridors leading to my childhood, a clear image emerged: a group of us being led into that room, where in the pool, ruddy-cheeked men, white hair on flabby chests, gold glinting on plump, manicured hands, leant against the tiled sides. Behind them, on the stone ledge, were bottles of wine and spirits. Smoke from fat cigars swirled above balding heads, and complacent laughter filled my ears.

Through the water I saw that the men were naked and those things that disgusted me so, those red things that could swell into something angry and hot, were bobbing between their legs.

'Well, well, some new little twinkles,' said one.

'Very nice, too,' said another, and more laughter broke out.

Just looking at them, with their flushed faces, their hands wrapped round cigars and glasses, nearly brought bile racing up to my throat. Even then I knew what they wanted, why we had been brought there. 'Nice men going to give you all some presents,' we had been told. But I knew what presents they were going to give us. They wanted the same as Colin Tilbrook.

'Let's get your clothes off now. Then you can get in the pool,' said one of the female wardens.

And children, too frightened to protest, obediently raised their arms for shirts and skirts to be pulled off, knelt down and untied shoes, peeled off socks until they stood, trembling with fear, clad only in their knickers.

'In you get,' the warden said. 'It's playtime.'

I wanted to scream out that I wouldn't get into that water. I wanted to run back the way we had come, but the warden's cold stare pinned me to the spot.

The eyes of one of the men raked my body and, through his sneering gaze, I saw myself: small, inconsequential, just a toy. His hand raised and his finger pointed at me. 'That one first,' he said. 'That little blue-eyed twinkle can come in my direction.'

'You first then, Madeleine,' said the warden, as she lifted me in.

Hands grabbed my shoulders, and gold from a wedding ring glinted up at me. 'Pretty little thing, aren't you?' He turned me round, held my body against his chest and bounced me up and down. I could feel that thing underneath my body, pressing against me, and just hoped he wouldn't ask me to touch it.

The warden picked up another small girl, 'Who wants this little naked twinkle, then?' And, laughing, another grey-haired man shot his hand up. Other men called out and received a sobbing child. The water churned as small bodies were pressed, stroked and pulled. Heads were held, tiny mouths protested, while men with grandchildren of our ages laughed, shouted and bucked.

Now I brushed a tear away; that image had been too real, too clear.

The voice of the policeman broke into my thoughts: 'So, you think you should retract that statement?'

I considered his question as a red blotch of anger stained my cheeks. 'You came to me. You wanted information.' As I uttered those words, thoughts of the harm those visits had done flashed through my mind. The questions of the police had opened a door to my past that was now impossible to slam shut.

A rift had been torn through my marriage. In bed, where once there had been closeness, there was now a space between us, filled with the secrets that I had never told. My family's confusion, about what they had learnt and their hurt that I had not been able to confide in them, showed in their eyes. And the childhood memories that had now escaped had metamorphosed, it seemed, into demons that swooped down nightly to torment me.

'Now,' I said, trying to control my anger, 'you're not happy with what I've told you.'

'Madeleine, have you heard of acquired memories?' asked the policewoman, not unkindly.

I remained silent, which she took to be a 'no'.

'Well, often, when an adult has therapy, part of their treatment is to recall childhood memories. Often, when those memories have been suppressed, hypnotic therapy is used. And we know you have had therapy.'

If that's what you want to call it, I thought angrily.

She took no notice of my discomfort, just continued with her textbook opinions. 'Events that have caused distress in earlier years can then be dealt with. And during those sessions, sometimes memories are accidentally imparted. The recipient believes them, so they are not lying when they repeat them. Do you think that could have happened to you?'

'No, it bloody couldn't have,' sprang to my lips, but before the words left my mouth, the policeman interrupted: 'I mean,' he said, ignoring her theory, 'I've been down there myself. Had to bend. No room for a grown man down there, far less ten of them. No room for a pool either. Now, let me just ask you something. You said it was businessmen down there, right? Businessmen, sitting in a pool. Now, you've told us you were placed in there. Was the water hot or cold? There's no sunlight down there, so without heating, the water would have been freezing.'

'I can't remember,' I answered.

'Well, then, here's a thought for you to dwell on. Would men of the type you've described sit in a shallow bath full of cold water? And, let's face it, if they had, I don't think they would have been able to get too excited, if you get my drift.

So I'm asking you again, Madeleine, do you think you should retract that statement?'

And, with visceral understanding, I knew what had happened.

I wanted to throw something at the police, rant and rave, yell accusations, ask them who had taken the bath out. For I knew, by looking at their implacable faces, that it was no longer there. 'But Graham Power believed it was there. He believed us. And I know there've been thirty victims of the home stating the same as I have.'

'Thirty "alleged" victims, Madeleine. There has not been any proof that those crimes were committed.' He paused. 'Anyhow, what Graham Power believes is no longer relevant. Seems he was a bit gullible where you lot were concerned. Swallowed everything you all told him. So he's been given a bit of a holiday. Stress got him imagining things.'

'When will he be back?' I asked desperately, but I already knew the answer.

'No date fixed for that,' was the answer.

This time, before I could ask any more, the woman said, 'Madeleine, do you think that the story was told by one of you and you all started to believe it? Could that be what happened?' she asked, playing good cop to his disbelieving one.

'You mean like group hysteria? No! Let me explain something,' I said, finding it difficult to keep my anger and my dismay at Graham Power's suspension hidden from them. 'The ones still in Jersey who were in that home rarely mix. And if we do meet, we don't talk about it. What do you think happens? That we have coffee mornings and see who can top the most terrible childhood story? We don't. We don't even want to think about our time there. Now I might get the size of a room or the height of a ceiling wrong and not be able to remember if the water was hot or cold. I was only five when I was sent there, and most of the time I was terrified. But I remember those men. I remember them all. And I am not going to give up. Someone will be made to listen to us,' I said, feeling my face redden at the fervour in my voice.

They said nothing more to me. After all it was beginning to seem that the case was nearly closed. With our main supporter suspended and his deputy, Lenny Harper, retired, who was left to hear us?

CHAPTER TWENTY-THREE

There was nothing left for me to do over the months that followed but to wait for the first trial. The Jordans were being brought back to Jersey. Although I had been told that Graham Power was on an extended holiday, I still hoped I would receive another phone call from him. Meeting him had given me confidence that at last our voices would be heard. Now I was convinced that this trial was only the first of what was to come. Others would follow, and those abusers would be made accountable for their crimes. We must have been believed, after all. That thought consoled me for what the opening of the inquiry had cost my family.

At some point my husband had gone. A good, decent man, had he left because he couldn't take any more? Or had I told him to go? I wasn't quite clear on that.

When the day came for the Jordans to face a prosecutor determined to see justice done, I and others like me made our way to the court. That morning I walked with buoyant steps and optimism in my heart. I took a seat on the hard wooden bench and waited. Eventually a door opened and I watched as two elderly people were led in.

My first thought was that, although Anthony Jordan was still a bulky man, dressed in a pale grey suit, he seemed utterly respectable. Where, I asked myself, was the coarse bully who had punched me so hard in the stomach that I had fallen to the ground? The man who had squeezed budding breasts and said, with a leer, 'Oh, you're going to grow up to be lovely, all right. No one would guess by looking at you where you've come from. Mind you, as soon as you open your mouth they'll find out you're nothing but trash.' A blast of bad breath would hit me as he laughed, twisting my nipple.

Morag Jordan, who had picked girls up by their hair and brought terror into our lives, looked so small and helpless. Just a woman approaching old age with a pale, lined face. Her eyes, which had scorned and mocked me, were now hidden by glasses, so I could not gauge her expression. I observed that she looked straight ahead and paid no attention to the room. There was arrogance in her demeanour.

The people I had known were hard to see in the couple my eyes were fixed on. Would they have recognised me if they had seen me in the street? Could they have stripped away the years to see past my middle-aged exterior to the girl they had tormented?

They must have known, I was sure, that some of us would be there. The ones who were not so damaged that appearing in public frightened them. Yes, they would have been aware that we were there to watch their downfall, hoping with every fibre of our being that they would be locked away for many years.

We understood that all prisoners hated those who had hurt children: would their lives be turned into a living hell as ours had been? I hoped so.

Yet when I looked at them, then glanced at the jury I felt a faint apprehension. It was not a cross-section of the poor and not-so-poor. It was a group of twelve people in which the men were wearing well-cut suits, gleaming white shirts and discreet ties perfectly knotted. The women varied from sleek and well-groomed to comfortable middle-aged. The one thing they had in common, I was convinced, was that none of them lived in social housing.

At last the charges were read out. Inflicting 'casual and routine violence' while working as house-parents at the children's home, said the prosecutor. He went on to outline how the pair had acted as 'intimidating bullies' while they had carried out 'frequent and callous' assaults on vulnerable residents. He stated that they had force-fed children, rubbed their faces in urine, locked them in the punishment cells for days on end . . . Those were just some of the offences, he told the jury.

Every day for two weeks I heard the defence barrister denying the Jordans' guilt. The couple had only done their duty in disciplining damaged and difficult children. He hinted that many of the inmates had, on their release, given nothing but trouble to the police. Did he, and others like him, believe that bad genes were the cause, not the system that had let them down so badly? I already knew that was the belief of many.

The prosecutor stated that the Jordans had grossly abused their power.

He called some of those who had suffered under the Jordans' regime. Damaged people who, with their lack of education, schooling and fragile self-esteem, were no match for the smoothness of the defence. I heard them stumble over their statements and saw the woman whose face had been rubbed in urine burst into tears. The jury's faces gave little away as, one by one, the witnesses did their best. There was no compassion in their expressions when tears fell or faces flushed scarlet.

Our ministers and priests tell us we are all born equal in the eyes of God, but I felt then that that was not how Haut de la Garenne's victims were seen in the eyes of the rich and influential. Eventually the case was summed up and the jury sent to reach their verdict. After deliberating for more than eight hours, the jury found them guilty on eight counts but acquitted Morag Jordan on a further twenty-eight counts and Anthony Jordan on four. Both defendants remained silent as the verdicts were read. They would be sentenced in January. Bail was set. They were free to go until then.

'So they can have Christmas as free people,' I muttered.

'Still,' said my son, 'they've been found guilty on eight counts. That's good, Mum.'

No, it wasn't.

At that moment I hated all those in authority. Had that defence barrister not seen the bravery of those people giving evidence as he tried his best to tear it apart? If he had, he'd decided to remain oblivious of it. There was no justice in that courtroom as far as I could see. The others and I consoled ourselves that January was not far away. The Jordans would surely be worried as to how long their sentence would be. It would spoil their Christmas if they believed it was their last before they were locked up for a very long time. That was what we told ourselves as we waited.

I sat at my kitchen table on 6 January, a bleak, cold day, listening to the cheerful voice of Chris Stone on *Jersey Today* as I waited for the hands of the clock to move. At last it was time to leave, and again the others and I walked to the court. Outside, groups of us huddled together, while the same cameramen and reporters buzzed around us. The doors opened and we filed in. As before, the benches were crammed.

There was utter silence when the judge started his speech of how he had come to the amount of time the couple would be sent away for. At least ten years, I prayed, my whole body rigid with tension. Then she said the words that, for a second, I could not comprehend. Nine months for Morag and six for her husband.

A collective gasp of dismay sounded in the court when the judge handed it down.

As Morag heard her sentence, I saw in her eyes, behind her glasses, a look of satisfaction but not of surprise.

It was too much for me. All those interviews, the digging into my memories, the nightmares that had been released, and for what? Pain shot through my chest and, in a burst of uncontrollable fury, I shot to my feet.

My son tried to stop me. 'Mum, don't,' he pleaded, but I was deaf to anything but the rage pounding in my head. I screamed out at the injustice of it. Shouted that they were all in cahoots and much worse. My anger had wiped out my self-protection. Still shouting, I was removed from the courtroom.

The policeman, the one who had questioned me at length, was there. 'A mistake, Madeleine,' he said.

And so it proved to be.

There was one man left who wanted to fight for us. He publicly stated he believed our statements: Bob Hill, the deputy in St Martin's parish. He refused to accept the findings of the so-called 'experts', who had been called in after Graham Power's suspension. He insisted that the areas, suddenly called voids, were, as we had said, cellar rooms high enough for grown men to stand, that building work done in the 1970s had lowered the ceilings. He had contacted me. He wanted to find the secret doors leading to the rooms where, as children, we had been taken. 'I know it was long ago, Madeleine,' he had said, 'but can you remember where they are?'

I replied that some things could never be forgotten.

There was one, I told him, behind the pigeonholes where our shoes were kept. Yes, there were others, and, yes, I could show him.

Then I received another phone call. 'It would not be good for you to go with Mr Hill,' a cold voice told me. 'It would not be healthy for your mind.' And, as I held the receiver in a hand suddenly grown clammy, a question came into my mind that made the back of my neck prickle with fear. How had this man known what was planned?

I never went.

I would have done but, as I had found, there are ways to make courage disappear.

CHAPTER TWENTY-FOUR

It was after the trial, after that last interview, that my world fell to pieces. First I was angry with myself. Why had my courage deserted me? I was hurt by the lack of justice given to us and, above all, I was frightened. Frightened by the deep depression that enveloped me. It was as though a damp, dark fog had wrapped itself around my limbs and curled around my mind. It obscured my vision of day-to-day living, visited me at night and woke me each morning with its mocking scorn at my futile efforts to live my life.

My drinking increased. The amount I consumed crept up daily. My best friend now came in liquid form. Every time it slid down my throat, the muscles I had been clenching relaxed. Now I understood my mother. 'I'll be careful,' I told myself. 'I can handle a few drinks. Just until this is over, until I feel a little better.' One excuse bled into another.

I flailed out at my children and my husband when he visited. Their needs were not as great as mine. Hadn't I given them everything? Now it was my turn, though I didn't know what for.

'No, you're not going out,' I said to my fifteen-year-old daughter who, looking pretty, was heading for the door.

'I am,' was her reply.

I can't remember what else she said to me, or I to her. After all, my liquid best friend was doing the talking. I'm sure she said she hated me before she burst into tears and ran out of the house. Engulfed in a rage that had little to do with her, I flew through the door and grabbed her arm. Her temper came up to meet mine. We fought. I had never hit my children when they were young but now I lashed out. Her gold chain caught in my fingers and, without meaning to, I pulled it. It bit into her neck. She screamed.

What happened next is a blur. I remember my son talking to me, trying to get us both to calm down, and my daughter disappearing back into the house.

Then the police, with blue lights flashing on their car, arrived. Someone must have called them but I didn't know then who it was. 'Drunk and disorderly,' said the policeman, with cold eyes. 'And assault, Madeleine. Assault of a minor. That means we're going to charge you.'

My arms were held as they started to march me towards the car. I heard my daughter begging them not to arrest me. It was her fault, she said, all her fault. She had started it. She needed her mother.

Her pleas fell on deaf ears. 'She's coming with us,' said the policeman. 'I'm not leaving her here after what she's done.'

'She's been under a lot of stress,' said my son. 'She needs rest. I'll look after her. Get her to bed. There won't be any more trouble.'

They didn't listen.

'You're going to spend time inside, Madeleine,' said the policeman, when we reached his car. 'Just like your mother did. You'll have a record that will follow you.' A hand landed firmly on my head and I was pushed into the back of the car.

They booked me, then put me into a cell.

'Now you can sleep it off,' the duty sergeant told me, and suddenly I was sober. They're just trying to scare me, I said to myself, as I lay down on the hard mattress. After all, my daughter had told them it was just a family thing. And if I was drunk, I had been in my own home. Well, all right, I had followed her out to the pavement, but that was almost my own home. Those thoughts whirled around my head until the amount of alcohol I had consumed made me fall into a restless sleep.

***

My solicitor and my son, the latter carrying a case containing a change of clothes, arrived in the morning. I was not going to be released, as I had hoped. The police were pursuing the case and I was to appear in court later that day, the solicitor explained.

'What? My daughter's pressing charges?' I exclaimed, feeling a wave of dismay.

'No,' the solicitor reassured me. 'She absolutely refused, Madeleine. In fact, she's been to the police and begged them again to release you. She told them it was just a family row and that it was mostly her fault, but they lost patience with her and told her to go away. In fact, they added that if she was incapable of doing her duty, they would do it for her.'

They had been called out and were going to press charges and that was all there was to it.

'What will happen now?' I asked, feeling a surge of panic.

'It's not really an offence that merits a prison sentence, Madeleine,' the solicitor told me. 'Just a slap on the wrist and maybe a fine. In fact, you shouldn't be here. Your daughter has told them it was her fault, that you just tried to stop her going out against your wishes.'

'Well, that's one way of putting it,' I said, 'but I was drunk.'

'In your own home. Hardly a criminal act.'

Notes were scribbled and reassurances given. Then the solicitor departed.

'It'll be all right, Mum,' said my son. 'I can't stay long, though. They only let me in to give you your things. I hope we packed everything you need?'

Then he was gone and I was left with fear blooming in my stomach. For what I had not told my son was that the solicitor's eyes did not send out the same message as his words. He might know that I shouldn't be there, but he had dealt with the police many times and understood what could happen.

One thing I was sure of: they wanted me taught a lesson.

The police let me shower and, looking in the mirror, I saw a pale-faced woman with dark shadows under her eyes. My head throbbed and I could still taste the previous night's alcohol. I splashed my face, smeared a little foundation under my eyes and tidied my hair, which the mirror told me, was sticking up in all directions.

I tried to remember everything that had happened the night before. Yes, I'd been angry with my daughter. Yes, we had fought, but why had the police arrested me? That part was a blank and I prayed that I hadn't threatened them, then wiped it out of my memory.

Still feeling nauseous, I changed into a pair of clean jeans. Maybe, I thought, I should have asked my son to bring something smarter, but jeans were what I was comfortable in.

I waited in that small room, where the walls closed in on me and my stomach churned until I vomited. The face of the policeman was floating in front of my eyes, his expression when he told me I would do time. As much as I wanted to believe the solicitor, his reassurance meant little to me.

I was taken to the court in a police car and, glancing through the windows as it pulled up, I thought that, with its grey, thunderous clouds, even the sky appeared angry. A hand grasped my elbow and I was led to where I would hear my fate.

This time there were few people on the benches. My crime was of little interest. Just my children were there for me. I had sent a message for my husband not to appear. I didn't want his pity.

The magistrate was a woman, Judge Bridget Shaw. I had read about her when she was sworn in, knew that she had replaced the former magistrate, Ian Christmas, a man holding a position of trust who had been convicted of fraud.

He had been found guilty and was waiting for his appeal to be heard. In the meantime, he was drawing his full salary. If I was found guilty, I would lose my job and there would be no pay packet. I hoped that she had a rebellious teenage daughter at home: she might just understand how our row had erupted. I just wanted the day to be over and to be back at home with my family. To add to my nervousness I had to wait while another case was heard.

A young man, clean-shaven with short hair, somewhere in his twenties, had been charged with driving while under the influence of a considerable amount of alcohol. When it was read out he looked slightly embarrassed, but not, I noticed, particularly worried. He was wearing light grey slacks, a dark blue blazer and a tie that I was sure had his university's colours on it. Everything about his appearance said 'establishment', as did his voice when he was asked to state his name. I noticed that his fresh face showed little of his excesses and felt his confidence when he answered questions put to him.

That man, I thought, had drunk just as much as I had before he'd got into his car. He was given a fine and had his licence revoked for twelve months. From the smile of relief on his handsome face, paying the fine was not a problem, or being restricted to public transport.

I kept telling myself that surely what I had done was not as bad as his offence. He had endangered lives; I had had a row with my daughter. For the first time that day I started to believe that maybe my solicitor had been telling the truth after all. That I was going to receive a slap on the wrist.

I watched as the policeman, who had taken me from my house, the one who had told me I was going to do time, was called to give evidence. He opened his note-book, cleared his throat, then read out his version of that night.

He described a scene that, even to my ears, sounded bad. He said that I was drunk, out of control and still shouting at my daughter, who appeared terrified when he arrived. Then he went on to describe the red marks on her neck where he stated a chain had been pulled tight. 'She's fair-skinned!' I wanted to cry out. 'A bump on the edge of a table bruises her.'

Comments were made about my daughter refusing to testify. No one said that maybe she was scared of the repercussions if she did, but I felt that opinion circling in the air.

I cannot remember the magistrate's summing-up of my offence, just that she called it common assault, made worse by the fact the victim was a minor. She sentenced me to a month in prison and, like the two people I had watched escorted out of the court room just a short time ago, I, too, was led away. Now I was going to be taken to the place where I would have to face my child-hood tormentor.

Before my transport arrived I was placed in a cubicle cell in the courthouse. It was so small I could hardly move. When I had been left in a cell the night before, alcohol had deadened my dread of being locked in. Without it, my fear of being confined in small places intensified. Beads of sweat trickled down my back and my heart pounded with what I knew was the beginning of a panic attack. I clenched my fists and closed my eyes, as I tried to ward off memories of the detention cells in Haut de la Garenne that were forcing their way into my mind.

'Please just get me out of here,' I kept whispering, fighting the urge to kick the walls and scream.

Through my growing terror I heard a voice saying I had visitors. I opened my eyes and saw my son and daughter. Oh, thank God, I thought. Anything to take my mind off those images.

The relief that they were allowed to see me before I was driven to the prison outweighed my shame at being there. My son, I could see, was shaken by the verdict. He, like me, had imagined us all leaving the court and going home.

It was my daughter, though, for whom I felt the most concern. Her face was ashen, her eyes red from fresh tears. The last drop of my anger against her – I had found out that it was she, in a fit of pique, who had called the police – evaporated. She tried to tell me how sorry she was, that she'd never meant them to come, that she hadn't understood what she was doing. She looked, I thought then, like she had as a little girl when she had turned to me trustingly to make better some little hurt. 'Where has that trust gone?' I asked myself, knowing that the answer was clear. 'No, darling. None of this was your fault. It was mine,' I told her, and the expression on her face was worth the effort it had taken for me to admit that.

A flash of memory of just the two of us together came into my mind. She had been around five and I had taken her to the beach. There was a stall selling candy floss and, against my better judgement, I had bought her some. 'Oh!' she had exclaimed, as the first bite dissolved in her mouth. 'It's like eating clouds.' Thinking of the sugar-induced hyperactivity that would follow, I just smiled at her happiness. For that is what mothers do: they put the happiness of their children first.

'It was my drinking that caused it,' I said. By that very admission I had started to acknowledge what I had denied before. Alcohol had ceased to be my friend and become my worst enemy. It was time to banish its control over me. 'And I love you,' I added.

I felt tired then. Too much emotion had been released in one day. It was almost a relief to climb into the prison van that took me on the short journey to the prison. In it, my fingers plucked compulsively at my jeans as my imagination ran riot.

The word 'warden' conjured up pictures of big-bosomed women with eyes as cold as flint stomping towards me, keys and truncheons dangling from thick belts and aggression spilling out of tight-lipped mouths. Other pictures were also pasted firmly in my mind. There would be a strip search the moment I arrived; a cold shower, when I would be forced to stand naked before them; I would be made to wear a scratchy grey uniform before being thrown into a dark cell and given foul slush to eat.

I could not have been more wrong. There were no truncheons. Neither was there a cold shower or a strip search. No warden had a small, tight mouth or used words of aggression. Instead, with a smile bordering on friendly, they quietly explained the rules. I could wear my own clothes and change into fresh ones after I had had a warm shower, which had curtains. At visiting times, I was told, I had to wear a red sash around my shoulders, which stated that I was an inmate, not a visitor. I could exercise in the yard, where we were allowed to smoke. Provided we had behaved well, we could watch television. I could hug my children when they arrived and when they left.

They took me to my cell and brought me a cup of tea. 'Seeing as you missed the afternoon break,' they said, as an explanation for their kindness.

As I got to know the wardens, they became friendly, protective even. They knew who I was and where I had spent my childhood. They said it was wrong that I had been sent there, that my solicitor should have pointed out that I had been giving evidence about Haut de la Garenne.

Although they could not discuss their feelings about Morag Jordan, they reassured me that they would do their best to keep us apart. I could, if I wished, eat in my cell and exercise separately from her in the yard.

One warden told me that Morag was denying the charges against her. She justified her actions by saying she had only done her duty. She kept saying that the girls in her care were the children of problem families and had been placed in the home because they were uncontrollable, unruly, promiscuous thieves. The boys she denounced as delinquents. Very few of the inmates believed her, the warden added. But, still, it was better if I was prepared. I think she meant they didn't want me to lose my temper, which would only have made my stay longer.

Over the time I spent in the prison, I heard snatches of the stories that Morag had tried to put about. She dripped poison into the ears of her listeners as she whispered her versions of events. Her final tale, I was told, was that I was in prison for violently assaulting my daughter. That I had tried to strangle her, a fifteen-year-old-girl, and she couldn't understand my being sentenced to just one month.

Prison, though, is a hotbed of unreliable gossip – boredom is a great fertiliser. Take a minuscule kernel of truth and watch it grow into something far more interesting. When it has been repeated enough times, it has become almost unrecognisable from its original form. I was asked if it was true that the politicians wanted the Haut de la Garenne case to end. Whether there had been cover-ups by those in high office, desperate not to have Jersey's good name tarnished. And were they going to deny much of what had been discovered? Would experts waive reports that discredited nearly everything Graham Power and many of us had stated?

To all of that I shrugged. I didn't have the answers.

The next rumour I knew to be true: that Jimmy Savile, friend of prime ministers and royalty, had visited the home. Now, he supported numerous charities so that on its own was not alarming. The fact that he denied he had been to Haut de la Garenne was. Maybe he had forgotten the photograph in the local newspaper showing him sitting with a group. Had he, the man who had said, 'I don't touch children,' done so?

The answer to that question I kept to myself.

Other rumours abounded to which the inmates thought I might have answers. That children had died there, and rich men had taken boys out on their yachts to have sex with them. Of course they wanted to know, too, what I had said in my interviews, which I had no interest in sharing.

My fieriness and refusal to be quiet, my threats that I wouldn't rest until justice was served, were the real reasons I was there, they said. It had been done to discredit me. It might be that I had annoyed the police, I admitted, but that was not why I had been sentenced. The judge clearly thought that I needed to be away from my daughter for a spell. After all, she was aware of who had made the phone call.

I spent more time in my cell, as I didn't want to be part of the gossip. I just wanted the truth to be disclosed and I began to make a plan. Somehow I was going to get the rest of my story down. I would draw with words the landscape that lived in my head. I had learnt how much the world had changed since I was a child and had tried to tell adults what was happening to us at Haut de la Garenne. I had felt the disbelief of some, and others had treated me as though I was making up wicked stories. Forty years later, victims of abuse are no longer frightened to come forward. Shame is no longer heaped on their heads. Society has learnt that when a child is forced to perform unspeakable acts, it is not the child's shame. That shame belongs to the perpetrators and the narrow-minded bigots who despise victims of abuse. I know there are people who think that today's victims might turn into tomorrow's monsters, but I also know that it rarely happens.

Yes, I have come across those who have been damaged and progress from abused to abuser. Most of us, though, want to be part of a relationship, have children and make happy and secure lives.

CHAPTER TWENTY-FIVE

She was there when I was shown into the common room. Those pale, cold eyes met mine and for a second I froze. She knew who I was.

She had been Morag Kidd when I'd first met her. With her dark blonde hair, plain features and trim figure, she was, I had thought then, ordinary. But I quickly learnt that that was one thing Morag Kidd was not. At first her mundane appearance had made us think she was no great threat. After all, she was not a big woman.

Forty years later I have words to describe her. They are not the ones we used in our early teens – 'fucking bitch', 'fucking cow', 'fucking evil monster' – which showed little imagination but expressed our feelings. My adult self has learnt to use different words, like 'sociopath'.

Her antisocial behaviour took the form of enjoying others' pain. She used her intelligence to devise different ways of inflicting it. And the tiny part of her that needed someone to grow old with found her soulmate when she met the thick-set, brutal Anthony Jordan.

Was their pillow talk about whom they had beaten, humiliated and, in his case, touched? When they lay together in bed did they make sleepy plans of new horrors they could inflict on us? Did they whisper words that drew pictures of bruised and broken children? And when they crept out of bed at night, to shine circles of light on frightened children in bed, was the smell of fear a powerful aphrodisiac?

I have sometimes wondered if it was she who thought of changing some of those so-called voids into cells. Cells she introduced me to within weeks of her arrival. It certainly took a warped imagination to design them so artfully.

Now, as I hovered in the doorway, I heard the guard whisper, 'Don't worry about her – she has no friends among us.' Those words sent a warm glow through me. I took a deep breath and willed the fear, which had been instilled in me as a child when even the sound of her footsteps caused me to quake, to disappear. What was important, I suddenly realised, was not that she knew who I was but that I knew who and what she was. I was no longer the frightened child she had done her best to destroy. I was now a person in my own right. One who had overcome so much. Hadn't I managed to put the past behind me, married a man who loved me and brought up two bright, well-adjusted children? Children who, until the police interviews had begun, had felt safe and secure.

I might be in prison for unruly, drink-induced behaviour, but it was not my name that was linked to the word 'monster' in the minds of Haut de la Garenne's former inmates. Her name, unlike mine, was splashed across the internet, where her sentence, its leniency, was considered an outrage. The comments in various chatrooms made no bones about the fury the public felt towards her and her husband. Thanks to the twenty-first century, the world had seen their photographs. When they were released they would have no place to hide. Certainly their neighbours would see them through different eyes. Inside the prison, I registered that I was now the stronger of us. She was older, frailer, with no allies, and that man, her partner, protector and ally, was, for the first time since they had met, not by her side. Our roles were reversed. Why had I not seen that before? She ought to be scared of me now.

Would I creep up in the showers and attack her when no one could see? Did the wardens dislike her enough to look the other way? Maybe I'd wait until we were in the yard, taking our daily exercise, then trip her up. The final power I had over her was words. I could tell the other women not just what she had been sentenced for but all the other details of her cruelty, which I had tucked away in my head. Most of the women in the prison had children and I had already learnt that some were not afraid

CHAPTER TWENTY-SIX

It was on my first night there that my determination strengthened to do more to raise awareness of what we had suffered. The police might not believe that much of what we had told them was true. They had suggested that stories had circulated and become imprinted on our minds as fact. People don't care about what they can't see. Make them believe, though, and it's the person convincing them of the reality of the horror under their noses whom they begin to dislike. Yes, there were people such as the Jordans who had been unnecessarily cruel. They accepted that. As they accepted that Colin Tilbrook was a child molester – they could hardly avoid doing so since his own stepdaughter had spoken out – and that some inmates had abused younger children. I'm sure they were embarrassed to learn of the visits to the home of the man who, for at least a decade, had attacked and raped both women and children, and to be told that while they searched the island for the creature nicknamed the 'Beast of Jersey' he was playing Santa Claus at Haut de la Garenne. But stories of orgies in hidden rooms, rich men in yachts and a famous celebrity all taking their pick of the children?

No. I had been told that while some politicians had instructed the police to wind this scandal up, others were still questioning whether or not it was true. If it was, they had stated that justice must be done. Even more people needed to come forward until so many voices were telling their stories that they could not be ignored.

Problems faced those who wanted to help. Many of the people who had once been in the home were too damaged to relive past horrors, while others, with their drink, drug and mental-health problems, would never make credible witnesses. Some, I knew, had left the island and did not want to be reminded of it.

'Talking about it, Madeleine, means reliving what happened and feeling my pain all over again,' one friend had said, when I'd asked her if she was going to make a statement. 'Nobody in England knows I was in that place and that is how it is going to stay. It's been all over the news and we can hardly open a newspaper without seeing reports on how we were treated. Do you think I want my kids to know that their mother had been little more than a sex toy for some of those wardens? I've never even told my husband. He might not think he was the first but there's a limit to how many he'd want to know about.'

'But none of what happened was our fault.'

'We know that, and decent men might feel sorry for people who have gone through what we have, but they can still be a bit funny when they find they've married one. No way am I going to tell him now. And our friends? You think I want to see pity on their faces? Well, I don't. What good will it do?' she continued. 'Half of those bastards are dead or disappeared by now.'

'It's not just for us but for today's children as well. The public might not like hearing what happened. Well, who would like to think they'd mixed with men who did those things? But it wasn't just us, was it? It was also kids who came before us, the ones who came after us and those who'll be placed in care in the future. There's nothing new about child abuse. What *is* new, though, is talking about it. Bringing it out into the open and stopping the bastards getting away with it. If we get some sort of justice then people in power will try even harder to catch them, and no children's home will exist without more regulations.'

'Well, maybe I'm being selfish but I'm not doing it, Madeleine. No way am I going to talk to the police. Have you such a short memory that you've forgotten what happened when we did?'

I had not but it wasn't a subject I wanted to linger on.

That conversation depressed me and put questions into my head when I found she wasn't alone in her reaction. Had I been selfish in agreeing to give evidence? I asked myself. Apart from the Jordans, what difference had it made? I hadn't even been called as a witness in their trial – and there was no doubt that my family had suffered because of it.

No, I told myself, it had been the right thing to do. There were still enough of us who thought like me, who wanted to scream out their anger at the murder of their childhood and demand to be heard. At some stage we would be listened to and believed. Of that I was sure.

I had to spend a month in what had turned out to be a fairly sympathetic environment and now I decided how I was going to use that time. The interviews had unlocked too many vivid, unwelcome memories and I wanted somehow to put them down on paper.

***

My son came to visit the day after I had arrived in prison. There were, I noticed, fresh lines on his face – a face that was too young to have them. My behaviour had caused them and I felt a wave of sadness. My fingers itched to smooth them out, but although I could hug him on arrival and departure, no other touching was allowed.

'How are they treating you, Mum?' he asked, almost before he had sat down. From his tone, he was clearly expecting to hear the worst. I told him I was all right, that the wardens were kind to me. That I had had time to think. I promised him then that I would not drink again. Or, at least, that I would not drink enough to get drunk. 'I'm not an alcoholic,' I said. 'I can handle this when I get out. I won't have to join AA. I can do it without help. I know that.'

'So do I, Mum. You were just trying to escape your nightmares. I think you've been pretty strong.'

'Can you forgive me?'

'There's nothing to forgive, Mum. We love you.'

I explained what I wanted to do while I was in prison. I'd eventually been diagnosed as dyslexic and found writing difficult so I asked my son to bring in a tape recorder. 'If I give you the tapes will you type them up for me? Some of my memories are so muddled and I just want to get them down in order. It's funny but the early ones seem clearer than the later ones.'

'Do you think you're up to this?' he asked. 'I mean, it won't put too much pressure on you?'

'No,' I said, 'it won't. This time it will be therapeutic.'

He smiled. 'Good for you, Mum, and the answer's yes.'

CHAPTER TWENTY-SEVEN

It's hard to talk into a machine, harder in many ways than speaking to a human. There are no questions to act as a prompt, no sound of paper being rustled, and no offers of tea or coffee. Neither was there the relief of lighting up a cigarette to give me thinking time. Smoking was restricted to the yard.

One of the most difficult things was placing those memories in order. After all, the ones that have had the most impact on our lives are the easiest to recall.

***

A memory that never leaves me is of Frances, and how she was then. Frances, my bright, cheerful protector when I was five, the girl who had put herself in front of me and incurred more wrath than I was aware of. I never spoke to the police about her. She is on the island now, a prisoner of her memories. There are the bars on her windows and locks on her door, not to keep her in, for that would be futile – she never leaves the house – but to keep the world out.

There are people who make sure she has food, shop for her, collect her social-security payments and deliver it to the ghost of the girl I had once known. When I had returned to the home the first time to discover she wasn't there, I had asked and asked where she was, but no one wanted to tell me. 'She'll be back,' was all I was told.

She hadn't run away. She'd been sent away.

I never knew the reason for her absence.

Would I have understood even if I had been told? I might have experienced sex but I had little knowledge of how babies were made. I was too young to have been in the classes where the facts of life were explained.

Eventually, when she did return, the girl I rushed up to so eagerly was no longer the Frances I knew. Whatever had happened to her since I had seen her last had dulled her once sparkling eyes, rounded her shoulders and taken away her courage. All she wanted was to be left alone. I tried to talk to her, to tell her how I had missed her, only to receive a shadow of her former smile.

It was as though our former closeness had never happened. For me, it was yet another loss. She was moved to a different dormitory and our paths seldom crossed. She was allowed to study in the evenings and at mealtimes she sat with the more senior inmates.

When she turned sixteen she left, as she had told me she would. She came to say goodbye to me. She had a job, she told me, working in a hotel in England. 'In the country,' she had added. 'I want to train as a reception-ist,' she told me. Then she was gone, with no address for me to write to.

Twenty years passed before I saw her again. By that time I was married, my past buried and my life as con-tent as I could make it.

CHAPTER TWENTY-EIGHT

Haut de la Garenne was no longer a home for children. Instead, in 1986, it was being portrayed as a police station in the TV detective series *Bergerac*. I had been enlisted to work on the catering trucks.

Starting early in the morning we prepared ongoing buffets – breakfast, then snacks, lunch, more snacks and dinner. If it was late shooting, we prepared even more. Food was what the cast wanted, and enormous mounds of it were what they got. At the end of the day our bags were full of leftovers: cold chicken, roast beef, rolls, cakes – there was enough for me to feed my family.

At first, when I had been offered the job, I was reluctant to spend days in the vicinity of that grim, grey building, but the need for a second income outweighed my doubts. The pay was good and there was a certain excitement in seeing the stars close up, even sometimes exchanging a few words with them. The bustle of the film crews, the numerous extras waiting to be called, not to mention the groups of people waiting for John Nettles to appear, driving that vintage red Triumph convertible, combined to give the place a completely different atmosphere from the forbidding one I remembered.

It was on one of those mornings when Jersey is at its most beautiful that I saw her. That day, the only wisps of white appearing on the cloudless sky came from planes carrying holiday-makers. They were, I was sure, peering out at the sparkling turquoise sea and planning their first evening's entertainment. All around me I could heard the trill of small birds and the hum of bees, as they flew towards wild flowers. The air was heavy with the scent of summer and, feeling a wave of contentment, I closed my eyes.

When I opened them, Frances was there. She was standing quite still, staring at the building where once we had been housed. From a distance of several yards I could see she looked older, no longer a girl. Of course she did, and of course she no longer was – two decades had passed – but I would have recognised her anywhere. My memories had never let go of her.

I hesitated. After all, what would we talk about? Our shared experience had not been happy. Haut de la Garenne was no longer a place where children were sent to suffer. Did I want to delve into the past? What had gone on there was not a subject I wished to reminisce about. But I couldn't turn away and, squashing my reluctance, I slowly walked towards her.

She saw me and it was too late for any indecision. Had she, I wondered, been searching for faces in which, peeling back the years, she could see some of the children she had once known? I knew I had changed far more than she had. Who doesn't when childhood is left behind? But my hair was still the same pale red blonde and I, who had been small as a child, was petite as an adult.

Then I was in front of her and, as the years fell away, a lump came to my throat. 'Frances, is it really you?' I asked, although I had no need to. 'It's me, Madeleine. Do you remember me?'

'Of course I do.' Any doubt I had had as to whether she would be pleased to see me, after all this time, disappeared the moment she spoke. 'How could I forget?' Her arms stretched out to encircle me.

I was briefly taken back to when I was a child and she had looked out for me. She had been so strong then. Now I held her at arms' length and looked into her face. There was fragility in it, a sadness that showed even through her smile.

'I was hoping I'd meet you,' she said. 'I wondered if you were still here or if you, too, had left.'

'I never left,' I said. 'Are you no longer in England?' That was all I could think to ask.

'No, I've come back,' she replied. Behind those few words I sensed there was a story, not a happy one, she wanted to tell me. I was right, but it was not that day we talked, or the next time we met.

I understood that she wanted to get to know the adult me, to separate that person from the child, before deciding if she could trust in a friendship that had begun and faded so many years earlier.

We met in coffee shops, on walks along the beach and at my home. She never invited me to hers. Neither did she take up my invitation for her to join all of us in a family meal.

It was several weeks after that initial meeting that I learnt some of what had happened to her. Little by little, a few sentences at a time, she told me her story. It was as though travelling back in time exhausted her, but then, when I'd heard it all, I understood why.

'You wanted so little to do with me when you came back to Haut de la Garenne,' I told her one morning, when she was perched on a stool in my kitchen. I had tried not to mention our childhood, but that day, while we sat sipping coffee, I couldn't stop myself.

She glanced at me but said nothing. Remembering my childhood hurt, I blurted out, 'You were the only person I wanted to see when I was sent back there. Those wardens wouldn't tell me why you'd gone, only that you were returning.'

'And I did.'

'Yes. But you were so different and I was too young to understand that something must have happened to make you like that.'

She said she was sorry, that she hadn't wanted to hurt me. 'I have to go, Madeleine,' she said, tapping out her cigarette with quick, jerky movements.

The expression on my face must have told her that I knew her departure was only an excuse to delay telling me why she had turned away from me. She paused by the door.

'Madeleine,' she said then, 'I know that if we're going to be friends I owe you an explanation. It's just not something I can talk about easily. But the next time I'll try to find the words, I promise. I owe it to you to make sure you understand it was nothing you had done.'

We met again a couple of days later. I was due to work the morning shift at the film shoot and when I'd finished she was waiting for me. We took mugs of coffee and sat on a low wall.

'Seems appropriate to tell you what happened here, where it all started,' she said, with an ironic smile.

'So why did they send you away?' I asked.

'I was pregnant,' she answered.

I'd been expecting that, but the facts of how it had happened were far worse than I had imagined. 'Who was the father?' I asked, expecting to hear the name of one of the men who had molested me.

'I don't know.' Then a torrent of words burst out. She told me how she had been gang-raped, not by adults but by the boys she had thought were her friends. 'They kept saying they knew about all the men Colin Tilbrook lined up for me, that I was nothing but a whore, and why could I not put out to them? Was it because all those rich men bought me presents? On and on they went, egging each other on. I knew I couldn't get away from them, knew what they wanted. I was in the same class as the ringleader, had even helped him with homework, but that night, when he met my eye, there was no shame at what he planned on doing. "We know you give out to all those old men," he said, his face flushed with a sort of savagery that I'd never seen on anyone before, not even those men Tilbrook gave me to. "It's our time now." I tried to tell them it wasn't my fault, those men. I hadn't wanted to go with any of them. I kept telling them I'd had no choice but they refused to listen.'

As she recounted what had happened to her that night, I saw it all, like a reel of film playing in my head. She'd stood there, much like a rabbit caught in a car's headlights. Sense had told her to run, but also that there was no escape.

The ringleader, the boy she'd thought of as her friend, had made the first move. His hand had shot out and, before she could utter another plea, grabbed her face. His fingers dug into her cheek so hard she couldn't move, far less scream. His voice deepened, to a rough growl. He'd sounded more like a man than a boy. 'Just shut the fuck up, whore.'

Her ears rang with the shouts of the other boys.

'Get her down, man,' one said.

'Down, down, down,' chanted the other three.

His knee pushed between her legs, his hand slid under her skirt and his fingernails scratched her skin. Then she was on the ground, her skirt hiked up to her waist, her blouse and bra pulled up to her neck. His mouth covered a nipple, nipped it hard between his teeth. A cry died in her throat as the hand holding her tightened until she thought he would break her neck.

His leg forced hers apart, and she felt him fumbling for his zipper. He forced himself into her dryness, plunged hard and all the time he sucked and bit her breasts and her neck. With a juddering howl he finished, lifted his head, and she saw his triumphant smile.

That smile made her want to curl up and die, she told me.

'Hey! You next,' he cried, to the next boy. 'She's nice and wet now, be an easy ride for you.' He rolled off her and the next one climbed on. Her legs were pulled further apart and then he, too, bucked away while another round of applause filled her ears. The other two followed, one after the other, but by then she was too weak to fight them.

Afterwards, when it was all over and they had disappeared into the shadows, she staggered to her feet. She wanted to get inside the building and hide where no one could see her. Somehow, with every part of her body aching, she straightened her clothes and walked to her dormitory.

She risked going into the showers, although bathing at any other time than that which the rota showed was strictly forbidden. The only vestige of luck she had that night was that no one saw her. She leant against the shower's wall and let the water cascade over her while she scrubbed away the smell of the boys. Then she crept into bed, pulled the blanket up to her chin and, with the boys' faces printed on her retinas, lay staring blindly into darkness.

The ache in her heart, she had told me, was even greater than the deep penetrating pain between her legs.

Tears had trickled down her face when, with her arms wrapped round her body, she confided in me about that night. 'So, Madeleine, now do you understand now why I have no idea who the father was? It could have been any of them. Or one of the men those boys taunted me with. Colin Tilbrook had quite a few men, who shared his interests, visiting. It was them he gave me to.' She shuddered.

Of course we both knew about men who liked their prey very young. Prepubescent children, in fact.

'Oh, those evil bastards love fondling smooth little bodies. Get turned on by seeing numb fear on faces that are just about to say goodbye to their childhood, good-bye to innocence and goodbye to trust. Those bloody perverts love that power. You and I met them, didn't we?'

I gulped. I didn't want to hear any more. Seeing me flinch, she laid her hand on my arm. 'I know you've worked hard at putting what happened behind you, Madeleine,' she said gently. 'I can understand if you don't want to hear any more. Maybe I've been selfish bringing up the past. I didn't think how painful it might be for you.'

'But you haven't managed to put any of it behind you, have you?'

'No.'

'Maybe after you tell me the rest you might be able to. It's worth a try, isn't it?' I waited for her to continue.

'I was older than a lot of the children in the home when they were abused. I was thirteen when I was introduced

MADELEINE VIBERT

to those men who arrogantly say that they never touch children. Yes, they do. Just not tiny ones. Girls of thirteen and fourteen, no matter how mature they look, are still children. They may have a woman's body, but that doesn't make it right to touch them, does it? They even have a name for their desires – nympholepsy. I was one of their nymphs. "Comes from Ancient Greek," one man told me. "It means an unbridled desire for young, beautiful girls." He seemed to think that by putting a name to it and using a word I had to look up in a dictionary made his acts excusable. Another one told me that what excited him – once he'd removed the clothes of a girl on the cusp of being a woman – was her small breasts, combined with narrow child's shoulders. Whatever they called it, it was children they liked fucking,' she said bitterly.

I remembered then how she had looked at that age. As a child I had thought that any adult who was kind to me was beautiful, but when I pictured Frances at sixteen, she really had been. I had seen a collection of David Hamilton's work, published as a book, in the seventies. As I saw photo after photo of semi-naked girls on the brink of womanhood, I saw something else. The collection was titled *The Age of Innocence*, but I would have retitled it *The End of Innocence*. One picture had reminded me of Frances. With her long legs and tiny

200

waist, the model appeared to have been even younger than Frances had been when she'd left the home, but the resemblance was startling. They both had slender necks and smooth faces, framed by long dark hair. The girl's face was pensive; I'd thought she didn't seem happy.

Frances's voice broke into my thoughts. 'They sent me to England, but when I got there the doctor said it was too late for an abortion.'

'What happened to the baby?' I asked, realising that she must have carried a child to term.

'I don't know. They wouldn't tell me. I only know he went to a family, but I never knew anything about them. I was told he would be well looked after. That was the very worst, Madeleine, having him and losing him. I had held him, breastfed him for six weeks, and then they took him from me. My beautiful, perfect little boy, whom I loved from the moment he was placed in my arms. I watched as his tiny lungs made his chest flutter in and out, stroked every bit of him and inhaled that baby smell. He fitted in my arms, and when he slept, I was just content to gaze at him. Those perfect little hands, those unbelievably delicate eyelids, the pale down on his head . . . He was still part of me. And then they took him away from me for ever. I didn't care who the father was. Not knowing made him just mine.

'I begged and begged them not to take him, but they took no notice. The forms for adoption had been signed, they said, a suitable family found. It was too late. They locked the door of my room until he was out of the house. I banged and banged on the door. They gave me a sedative. When I woke it was to the realisation that he was gone and I would never find him.'

As she came to the end of her story, her body crumpled with the anguish of a mother who has lost her child. I waited. There was more to come, I knew.

'And then you came back to the home?'

'Yes. They made me promise not to talk about it. If I kept quiet, I would be left alone. I was afraid of them. There were stories then of girls disappearing. Maybe they had run away or, like me, become pregnant and been sent away. As well as being scared, my hormones were all over the place. All I wanted was to be left alone. I didn't want to answer questions, not then. I think if I had let myself cry I would never have stopped.'

'No wonder you changed,' I said. 'But I still don't understand what brought you back here after you'd left the home and gone to England. I should have thought you would never have wanted to set foot on the island again.'

'One of the boys in the home, Stephen Burns, left at almost the same time I did. We kept in touch, wrote letters, and then he came over to see me. We ended up living together for a bit. I thought then that, like you, we could put our past behind us and find some peace. We actually did get married. A register office, a couple of mates, and there we were, a married couple.'

'And? I mean, did you separate? What happened?'

'He's dead,' she said bleakly. 'Drug overdose. He was such a sweet person, but he was never quite right. He should never have been in that home. He had never done anything wrong. It was just that his mother had left, run off with some man, and his dad couldn't cope. He was cheeky once too often to the police. That was all but, no matter, into Haut de la Garenne he went. He was a pretty child, and being pretty in that place was a curse. Those rich men, who took the boys out in their yachts, bloody raped him. He was a messed-up kid when I knew him in the home and a messed-up adult when I married him.

'Anyway, his dad died not long before that. He never knew what his son had been put through, and Steve never wanted him to. Anyhow, he had his own house and he left it to Steve, plus a bit of savings. Actually made a will so that wife of his never got a penny. And now it's mine. That's why I came back.'

'You could sell and move,' I said.

'I'm not going to do that. Moving won't help. Can't escape from yourself, can you, Madeleine?'

I had no answer to that.

Weeks went by when I didn't see Frances. I feel guilty about that now, but I had two small children and my days were full of washing, ironing, cooking and worrying about making ends meet. Then, when she entered my mind, she would suddenly appear at my door. It was maybe a couple of years after our first meeting that I noticed her growing not aloof exactly, but detached.

'I saw him,' she said one day, as though I would be immediately aware of whom she meant.

'Saw who?' I asked, thinking she meant Colin Tilbrook, then remembering that he was dead. A fact that had caused me no grief when I had heard.

'One of the boys. The ringleader. He recognised me all right.'

'What did he do?'

'Just smirked.'

'Are you sure it was him?' I asked – he would look very different now. But she refused to accept it might have been just a man looking at a pretty woman.

That was the beginning of her not wanting to leave her house alone. At first I thought nothing of her ringing me up asking when I was going shopping so she could come with me. It was when I sensed her nervousness, as she thought she had seen someone she knew, that I knew something was wrong. If she heard a burst of laughter, she clutched my arm while she glanced surreptitiously around to see where it had come from. She must have thought it was directed at her, that wherever she went, behind her back, people were pointing fingers.

I persuaded her to go to her doctor. She was diagnosed with anxiety and depression. Drugs were prescribed. For a while I thought she was improving, but I was wrong. Her fear increased, until nearly every time we went out, she thought she saw someone from her past.

I tried to tell her that her fear was irrational. So many from the home had left Jersey, while several of those who had stayed had buried their secrets in alcohol. It had killed some who had become addicted to it.

The wardens who had abused us were now old and the worst of them was dead.

Sometimes Frances would appear completely rational, but that didn't last for long. She had therapy. I have no idea what was said in those sessions, but they seemed to help her. Until she said that cars were trying to mow her down. A short spell in hospital followed. 'I know it's all in my head, Madeleine,' she told me, once she was released, 'but knowing it doesn't make it any easier when I open my door. It just feels so dangerous out there. I try to move my feet, make them cross the threshold, but they refuse to obey. I just can't do it unless someone is with me.'

A small group took her out. Until the day came when she refused to leave. That must have been ten years ago. Her garden, which she'd loved, became neglected. A neighbour's son mows her small lawn. Her hair, once so thick and dark, has turned grey and her beauty faded. I think with sadness of the girl she was, so plucky when she stood up for me,

I hear her voice, an echo of who she used to be: 'As soon as I'm sixteen I'll leave this place. I'll make a new life. I'll be free.'

CHAPTER TWENTY-NINE

She didn't know, when my eyes rested on her, that I wanted to bring back images of events that had happened over forty years ago. Her flesh might have become slack, her bones more brittle and her face creased with a network of lines, but those eyes, with their malevolent stare, had remained the same. Just seeing her helped me search through my layers of buried memory and find the first ones of the couple we'd known as the Jordans. The first bad ones, I mean, the ones that told me just who they really were.

Like shaking a kaleidoscope, picture after picture came into my mind's eye. I could see her prowling the corridors and the dormitories, shining a circle of blazing light onto our beds, hoping to find one of us talking. Just the sound of those footsteps was enough to silence us and make us quake with fear.

She had very quickly done more than just instill that emotion in us.

Morag Kidd had submerged us in it, so much so that we never felt safe. Both she and her partner, Anthony Jordan, who soon became her husband, had innumerable ways of inflicting pain. A hard-bristled hairbrush thwacked harshly on the back of a head, a fragile arm twisted to breaking point, an ear pinched, a foot stamped on, a tiny finger being bent, a fist sinking into a stomach.

Those were the acts that hurt us physically, but there are many different types of pain and she made sure we experienced them all. There is the pain of humiliation, and she was a master at inflicting that. In my mind, I saw again that child, whose fear had caused her to wet the bed, having her face rubbed in the urine. I heard her being called a stinking little girl, then being sent to the laundry to wash her sheets.

I heard Morag's harsh northern accent ridiculing children as they entered adolescence, calling them spotty, stupid and lazy. She had a knack of identifying exactly how to strip away their every shred of confidence.

One girl, who had started her periods and was almost doubled up with stomach cramps, was told in front of the whole dormitory that she stank of blood, then two sanitary towels were thrown at her.

That type of behaviour was far from unknown in the home, but the Jordans added another dimension to the cruelty so carelessly inflicted upon us. They planned meticulously how to make us suffer most. Morag, especially, could sense our weaknesses and fears and in a very short time had worked out what was important to each of us.

The ones in the home who cared about nothing, or so they said, who were just counting the days, months or even years until they were free, and had no one outside to visit them, those who showed the sullen defiance of the unhappy, she made to feel even more unwanted and unloved. They were taught that they were without a future and life would never improve.

In my case, though, there was someone I loved unconditionally, and that was my mother. I understood that life had damaged her, while alcohol had taken away her ability to look after me. But I was not in the home because she didn't love me, which Morag tried her utmost to make me believe.

'So your little brother is still with your mother, is he? Guess that step-father of yours didn't want another man's child under his feet,' was one of her taunts.

'No, he's nice to me,' I told her, thinking, the first time she said it, she felt sorry for me.

'Well, maybe he's a little too nice to you and perhaps it's your mother who doesn't want you at home. Doesn't want him to be tempted by the sight of a young girl wandering around the house while she's getting older. Heard you all slept in the same room at their old place, too. Interesting!'

The heat would come into my face as those mocking eyes met mine.

'Why, I do believe you're blushing, Madeleine,' she said, chuckling.

My hatred for her took root then. She was trying to take away my belief in Frank's and my mother's love. Did she know that it gave me the strength to deal with much of what happened to me in the home? I think somehow she did.

Observing me almost shaking with the effort of controlling my impotent anger, and encouraged by my reaction, she poisoned her barbs with even more venom. 'Heard your mother prefers drink to you, Madeleine,' she would say, causing a tingle of rage to crawl up from my stomach and lodge in my throat. Each time I swallowed the words that threatened to burst out and used the only weapon I had: silence.

'Hmm. Cat got your tongue?'

I knew, by the way her lips tightened, that she was frustrated by my lack of response. She wanted me to lose my temper and answer her back so she could mete out a punishment far in excess of the one fitting the crime. I clenched my hands and lowered my head to escape looking at her. Each time she tried to chip away at my belief in my mother and Frank, I told myself that I was wanted. I knew I was. I must never let her succeed in making me think otherwise. I was in the home only because my mother was ill.

However, I proved no match for the scheming and vindictive Morag Jordan. I grasped this on the day when, thrown into the detention cells, I saw the gleam of triumph and satisfaction in her eyes. She had closely studied me, as she had all the others. She had learned my weaknesses and what was important to me. The taunts that came in my direction had the same theme. I was unwanted.

Finally, when she repeated yet again that my mother was a good-for-nothing drunk who didn't want me at home near her husband, something inside me snapped. I couldn't keep my mouth shut any longer. With my shoulders back and my cheeks flushed, I glared at her. 'That's not true,' I told her hotly. 'My mother loves me. That's why she takes the bus here and walks up the hill whether it's raining or hot. I'm not with her and Frank because she's ill.'

I had made a mistake with that outburst; one that proved to have dire results. I had not worked out at that stage that feeding Morag any information gave her what she needed to select her weapons. Now she had a snippet of personal information to investigate and manipulate to her advantage.

For a short time she appeared to have forgotten about my mother and I began to believe that she had accepted what I'd said. She was almost pleasant to me on a couple of occasions and, regrettably, my guard slipped. Lulled into a false sense of security, I had no inkling that she was just planning her next manoeuvre.

For Morag, as I was to learn, did not take kindly to being thwarted. She was going to see to it that on my mother's next visit I would, by my behaviour, let her down. I was going to regret that outburst, all right. Not only had I shown how protective I felt towards the woman who, because of circumstances and weakness, had been unable to have much to do with my upbringing, I had also uttered the word 'ill'.

Morag must have made it her business to find out what form that illness took and discovered that my mother was asthmatic. For her, the uphill walk to the home would be considerably more tiring than for others. And if, when she arrived, she was turned away because of my bad behaviour, she would have to face the walk back without the benefit of any recuperation time. Knowing that I was responsible for causing her distress would hurt me even more than it might affect my mother.

Yes, Morag and I were in a battle: she was determined to break me and I was equally determined to protect the core of who I was.

She won when she threw me into the detention cells.

Once I was in that tiny room, where only she could say how long I would be left there, I was completely in her power, a fact of which we were both aware. It was there that I understood how cleverly Morag had orchestrated the events that had led to my punishment.

She had executed a scheme that she and her thuggish husband had, most probably, spent an enjoyable hour or so planning. And, I thought angrily, I had played right into their hands, although it's difficult to imagine even now what I could have done to make the outcome any different. At that age, for I was not quite eleven, I was no match for a woman like Morag. Once she had planned to make someone suffer, nothing was going to stop her.

Over the time I knew her I watched her plot against and manipulate everyone. Like a spider, she spun her web, and waited for her prey to become ensnared in its almost undetectable strands. Then, when there was no way for her victim to escape, Morag would smile triumphantly. Waving her justification for their punishment in his or her face, she took obscene delight in informing the unfortunate child just what was in store for them.

Locking the so-called culprit in the cells was a method she instigated and she took particular pleasure in handing out. It was also the one we dreaded most. Those bleak, small rooms were beneath the floors in what we called the cellars. I had heard other girls whisper that just a few days down there would turn even the bravest of us into a sobbing, shrieking mess. No other punishment was feared as much as being locked down there. Just allowing the memory of that day to surface was enough for me to travel back in time to when I was, as I said proudly then, nearly eleven. It is as though I'm looking into a mirror at the childhood me.

My face is puffy with tears and I'm shivering with cold. The only furniture in the cell is a wooden box with just a wafer thin mattress on it. No bedding or pillows, just a worn blanket in which I've wrapped myself. My eyes are shut. I don't want to look up at the large window, without curtains, which was at ground level. Through it, the outside world is visible, but so, of course, am I.

I'm imagining that already people are staring in and I ask myself how long I'll be left there, and fight the urge to pee. There's a bucket in the corner. I saw it when I was put in here, but the thought of someone at street level watching me squatting on it is unbearable. I just want it to be dark so I can be invisible.

If, when I had woken up, I had thought that this might happen to me, I would not have forgotten, just for a few moments, where I was and who controlled us but I had and here I was.

It was a Saturday morning, which meant no school, something that always made me feel happier. Outside, the sun was shining and I, along with two friends, was desperate to go into the grounds to play hide and seek or jump over a skipping rope.

As soon as breakfast was finished and our dishes cleared away, we caught each other's eye and headed for the door. I was hoping my mother would come and take me out. She had told me she would try.

'It isn't that I don't want to see you, Madeleine,' she had said on her previous visit, curling her fingers round a lock of my hair. 'It's just that I'm not as well as I was.'

Poverty and cigarettes had taken a toll on her, which even I could see. Winter and summer, she was plagued with a chesty cough, her ankles were swollen, and I knew they ached when she made the journey up the steep hill to visit me. But she always assured me it was worth it, just to see my face. During that visit, though, she had admitted that she might soon find coming to the home too difficult.

I had felt a surge of fear. I asked her what was wrong and she explained about the asthma. She blamed the damp in some of the run-down places where she had lived. 'I get so short of breath,' she had told me. 'I've good days and ones not so good. And walking up that hill can be difficult. The doctor has told me to give up smoking, but I can't give everything up, can I, Madeleine? I mean, it's my one bit of enjoyment.'

She didn't look well, and I could hear her wheeze with each breath she took. But still, with a child's optimism, I hoped today was a good one for her and that she was still coming. Morag would know, for visitors had to have permission to come, but I didn't want to ask her because I knew she would use it against me.

All I could do was wait.

I knew that if my mother was coming, it would not be until later in the day and I didn't want to spend time in the common room, when the beams of sunlight were beckoning us to pick up a skipping rope and play on the grass.

As one, without a word being spoken, my two friends and I made a beeline for the outside door. Just as we were in the long corridor leading to it, a harsh voice stopped us in our tracks. 'Where do you think you're going?'

This was a question that my friends had the good sense to let me answer.

'Outside, miss,' I said, thus sealing my fate for what was to happen next.

'Well, did any of you ask me? No, of course you didn't, Madeleine.'

My heart sank. She had just added another rule to her ever-growing list. In fact, I thought, she had probably only thought of that one when she had seen us heading towards the grounds.

Those pale eyes, gleaming with malice, were now fixed on me, as she waited to hear what excuse I could think of. Standing up straight, I forced myself to meet them and not show how scared I was.

'I didn't know we needed to ask on a Saturday, miss,' I said, as firmly as I could. That small act of bravery did me no good whatsoever.

'Not even an apology, Madeleine? What an insolent girl you're becoming. Now, do you know what the cure for insolence is, Madeleine?'

'No, miss.'

'It's work, Madeleine. Work is character-building. It's only in the dictionary that "success" comes before it. Not, of course, that you would understand that. Not with what I have been given to understand about your lack of reading skills. I hear a six-year-old can do better than you. Luckily, I'm not your teacher. But it is my job to help form your character. So I have a nice little chore for you. Follow me, your little friends, too – no doubt it was your idea, but they went along with it.'

Dismally, we trooped behind her as she led the way to the main entrance hall. 'I want the whole of this, and the corridor you were racing along, scrubbed. I think, today, you can forget about using the machine,' she said, referring to the large metal contraption that was normally used by the boys. 'It's far too heavy for you, so you'll have to do it by hand. There are the brushes you can use,' she said, pointing to several scrubbing brushes neatly laid out beside a stack of pails. The sight of them filled me with rage. She had decided that we would spend the day inside before she had seen us.

Intuitively, I knew there was more to come and any self-restraint I had disappeared. I was unable to stop myself showing the resentment I felt and glared at her.

'Do you have a problem, Madeleine?'

'No, miss,' I answered, in the most dutiful tone I could muster.

'Good! Now, how long do you think it will take you girls to complete this task?'

'Don't know, miss,' was the only answer we could give. Looking at the size of the brushes, which were just big enough for both our hands to grasp and to ensure that the work would take several hours, it was not a question we could answer.

Seeing she was waiting for one of us to speak I replied hopefully, 'By lunchtime, miss.'

'Well, I do hope so, Madeleine. Your mother is coming then. She rang this morning. It's such a long walk from the bus stop and, with her being asthmatic, well, I believe she finds it very tiring. So it would be a shame if, because of your bad behaviour, she has to be turned away.'

'Yes, miss.' Tears pricked the back of my eyes. She wasn't going to let me see my mother, however quickly we worked. Of that I was certain.

'Well, you'd better make a start, Madeleine, hadn't you? No time to waste. I'll be around to inspect your work. In the meantime, I trust you not to talk. Utter silence makes work go faster and it's good for the soul as well.'

There was nothing we could do except walk to the kitchen, fill up our buckets, one with warm soapy water, another for rinsing, and, arms straining under the weight, carry them back to where we were to start scrubbing.

With the picture of my mother struggling up the hill in just a couple of hours, I clenched my teeth and moved the brush up and down as fast as I could. The others, maybe ashamed that they had not owned up to being equally as guilty as I was, were also putting in serious effort. If we finished by lunchtime perhaps they'd be able to go outside after all.

As none of us had a watch, I don't know how long it took to clean the hall – I think about an hour. Knowing she would be looking for any excuse to detain us, I inspected it carefully, searching for the tiniest speck of dirt, but it appeared that every bit was now spotless.

When we started on the corridor we each took a section. My hands ached with holding the brush, as did my arms, legs and back, and my face was sticky with perspiration, but nothing was going to make me slow down. As I brushed a strand of hair away from my hot cheeks a shadow fell over me. I knew, without lifting my head, that it was Morag Jordan.

I kept on rhythmically moving the brush, my eyes staring at the grey granite floor, glistening with soapy water, willing her to go away, which clearly she had no intention of doing.

'Well, now, haven't you been working hard, Madeleine?' she said, in a voice too sweet to trust. 'You've almost finished. You really want to see your mother, don't you?'

I nodded and gave her, against my pride, a pleading look. Oh, please, just say I've done enough and let me go, I begged silently.

I should have known that was never going to be her intention.

She moved fast, giving me no chance to hold on to the bucket. I saw her foot rise and heard the thump, as she kicked it over, and I saw the stream of dirty water running across the section I had just finished. I looked up then to meet those cold pale blue eyes. 'Careless girl, aren't you, Madeleine? Well, you'll just have to mop it up with this,' and she threw down a sponge. 'It shouldn't take you too long. But, I'm sorry to say, too long for you to see your mother. I'll just have to explain to her that, even though you knew she was coming, you still acted badly enough for me not to allow you visitors. She'll understand that we can't reward bad behaviour, won't she? Just think, Madeleine, she's on the bus now. Soon she'll be getting off and walking up the hill. And it's a very hot day. Such a shame she'll have had a wasted journey.'

Out of the corner of my eye I noticed that my friends were keeping their heads down and continued to scrub. They knew better than to offer to help me. I can't say I blamed them. If they'd appeared to be taking my side it would not have lessened my punishment, only increased theirs.

'Well, Madeleine, are you just going to look at that dirty water or are you going to clean it up?'

Heat suffused my body as a fierce rage shot through it. A little voice inside me was saying, 'Just do it, Madeleine. Say nothing and clean it up. Don't rile her. She wants you to.'

Another voice, louder than the first, shouted, 'Tell the bitch to get lost.'

'No,' I said. 'Not with that sponge. You knocked it over, miss, not me.'

A triumphant smile lit her face and I knew that burst of temper was exactly what she'd wanted. If I could have, I would have swallowed those words back down, apologised and begged her to let me see my mother. But it was too late for that.

'Rude, insolent and a liar as well,' she said. 'You leave me no other option, Madeleine, than to put you in the cells. A spell down there will soon cool that temper of yours. It'll make you think about the consequences of being disrespectful. Now, stand up. Your friends can clean up your mess.'

I couldn't. The words 'cells' had sent fear crawling up my spine and my brain was having trouble telling my limbs to move.

She laughed, reached down, entwined her fingers in my hair and yanked it so hard that she pulled me on to my toes. The pain shooting across my scalp was almost unbearable, I thought she was going to pull it out by the roots and then the pressure released. Her back-up had arrived. Anthony Jordan and another female warden positioned themselves on either side of me.

'We're going to take this troublesome miss down to the cells.'

My arms were caught and I was half carried, half dragged along the corridors to a flight of steep stairs, cunningly concealed behind the cupboards where we stacked our outdoor shoes.

'Down you go,' she said and, knowing she was quite capable of pushing me, I did as I was told. Again my arms were taken in a hard grip. What did they think I could do against them?

It was cold and dark down there. I heard a key turning in a lock, a door opening, and I was propelled into a small room, with the three adults following me. The space was almost too small to contain us all and I could feel their breath on my face.

'Get her clothes off,' Morag instructed. 'This one needs to learn a little humility.'

The female warden moved to lift my dress.

'No, let him,' said Morag, nodding towards Anthony.

With a knowing smirk, he bent down and took hold of my hem. 'Hold her arms up,' he said to Morag, and my dress was pulled over my head in one slick movement. I was left standing in my vest and knickers.

'I think the rest better come off. What do you think?' she asked him.

'Oh, I think so. This one's trouble, all right.'

I forgot my pride then, forgot I'd made a pact with myself never to beg, never to cry in front of those bullies. The shame of a little girl, not quite eleven, drove that away. Tears ran down my face as I begged her not to do it. Words like 'Please, I'll be good, I promise,' came out of my mouth, but none of them were to any avail.

'You should have thought of that before, Madeleine.'

And, to add to my humiliation, their faces showed gloating satisfaction.

It was she who yanked my knickers down, but not before she had pulled them up as high as she could so that they cut into me. It was he who pulled my cotton vest over my head and I felt his fingers running across the back of my neck.

'Here's a blanket,' she said, throwing it at me. Then, gathering up my clothes, they left me in that small, cold room, locking the door behind them.

***

I was there for more than forty-eight hours.

CHAPTER THIRTY

In July the headlines of every newspaper were about the capture of Edward Paisnel, the man I had known as Uncle Ted, the so-called 'Beast of Jersey'. On street corners, in pubs and shops, small groups of people gathered to whisper gory details about the man who had terrorised the island for over a decade. He was the monster of nightmares, a creature wearing iron-studded wristlets and a hideous rubber mask. A mask which hid a face that, when finally uncovered, was almost as terrifying as the artificial one.

Unbelievably, he had crept undetected into people's houses for eleven years. Initially he attacked only women, but as his confidence and depraved appetites grew, he started abducting children. Threatening to cut his victim's throat if they screamed, he led them into the woods and fields where he abused, raped and sodomised them. After he had finished with the children, almost as though he was mocking the authorities, he led them back to their homes. In some cases he told them to go to sleep before he disappeared into the darkness.

It seemed impossible that out of a population of less than ninety thousand, on an island measuring only seven miles by twelve, no one on Jersey guessed his identity.

During his horrendous reign, I doubt there was one family not terrified of the man whom no one had managed to describe sufficiently well for the police to compile an identikit picture.

The close-knit community of Jersey, who, until the man in the mask arrived, had had no reason to doubt their neighbours, now locked and bolted their doors and kept their children close by. There must have been suspicious glances, not just at strangers but at anyone whose lifestyle was slightly unusual or even solitary but, at first, it must have been unthinkable that such a monster was an islander. With the first three attacks, all on women, taking place in November, though, when the last of the holiday-makers had left, the growing fear that a local man was responsible spread across the island.

After those three attacks, there were no more for at least a year. People began to think the man had left Jersey, driven out by his notoriety. 'Must have been an outsider,' they said.

But early in 1960, he crawled through a downstairs window, climbed a flight of stairs and abused a ten-year-old girl. He had planned the attack carefully, luring the father away from the house. He was gone for just a short time, but that was all it took.

'It wasn't the same man,' the police said, as the words 'serial rapist' spread, with outrage and fear, around the community. 'The other victims were adults. This must be an isolated case.' A statement they had to retract.

The next victim was a twelve-year-old boy and the one after that a young woman. Any doubt that only one man was behind the atrocities disappeared when all three victims described the mask he had worn.

The pressure was on for Jersey's police force, and experts from Scotland Yard were brought in. A fisherman, Alphonse Le Gastelois, was arrested and released without charge but had to flee the island. People wanted blood and, unable to lay hands on him, they burnt down his home.

Then the monster struck again and again.

It was nearly eleven years after the first offence that he was caught, not by brilliant police work but because he jumped a red light and, seeing the police car behind him, tried to outrun it. This time there was no doubt the police had the right man. The items found in his car, a rubber mask and a pair of studded wristlets, were evidence enough. As was his coat: its shoulders were embedded with sharp nails to pierce the hand of anyone who tried to either fight or apprehend him.

There were celebrations when people heard the news. The feared prowler was going to be charged on thirteen counts. But, as the television newcaster said, who knew how many had never reported being dragged from their beds and molested?

When first I heard about the monster's capture, I was sitting on the couch, between Frank and my mother, watching the news on our small black and white television. A young man, microphone in hand, was telling viewers about the car chase that had resulted in the capture of the most feared man on the island. His voice rose as he painted the picture of two determined police officers giving chase along the coast road and how they had finally apprehended the Beast of Jersey, whom the islanders had come to believe was invincible.

Frank and my mother were watching so intently that they were oblivious to the fact that I was staring at the screen and listening to every word. As his name, Edward Paisnel, was given and his picture flashed up, I froze. I recognised him. Gripping my mother's hand, I squealed.

'Whatever's the matter, Madeleine?' my mother asked.

'I know him – that's Uncle Ted!' I exclaimed, almost stuttering in my haste to get the words out.

My mother paled. 'What are you saying? How could you know a man like that?'

'He comes to the home,' I said. 'His name's Edward, but we were told to call him Uncle Ted.'

Frank got up and switched off the television, then turned and looked me in the eyes. 'He came to Haut de la Garenne, Madeleine? Why? What was he doing there?'

'He was our Santa Claus.'

Silence fell and, nervous, I tried to fill it. 'He's often in the home. I don't like him. He's so ugly and he stares. But he and Mr Tilbrook are friends. So I suppose he comes to visit him,' I babbled, hoping they would start talking about something else.

'You mean he's been visiting that place ever since you've been in there?' asked my mother, looking a bit sick. 'Did he ever touch you? You know – there?' she asked, pointing towards my crotch in case I hadn't understood what she meant.

I felt like screaming, 'Why is that so important? You know others have. Why would it be any worse if it was him?' But even then I understood that when my mother had a problem she couldn't deal with she pushed it so far to the back of her mind that it ceased to exist.

'No,' I said instead. 'I only saw him when he was dressed as Santa Claus. It was when I was smaller. He sat me on his knee and asked if I'd been a good girl and what I wanted for Christmas. Because I knew what his face really looked like, I was just pleased that the fluffy beard he'd stuck on hid most of it. But I could see his eyes and they scared me. I just wanted to get away from him.'

'But you're sure he never hurt you? Never did anything bad to you? Madeleine, this is serious,' said Frank.

I felt cross. I didn't want to be reminded of the time when I'd told them what happened in the home, or hear their excuses as to why they had done nothing about it. And, even more importantly, have them say that they didn't believe me. Because I was sure that they hadn't allowed themselves to accept what I'd told them. Otherwise why had they not acted? My mother had said they would take me away from her permanently if she did, but they had done that anyhow, hadn't they?

All the old hurt and my disappointment in my mother and Frank rose in me. If they weren't going to protect me, who else would? Why be upset about this new revelation? But all I said was 'No, I told you. Not me, but I heard he hurt some of the boys.'

'Oh, my God!' my mother exclaimed. 'I just can't believe he was allowed in there. Not after what's come out about that monster.'

'What?' I asked, wondering if he'd done anything worse than I had already seen, only to be told it was not suitable for children's ears. That made me more determined to find out.

Over the next couple of weeks, gleaning as much information from other children as I could and eavesdropping, I put together the shocking truth of what kind of man Uncle Ted had been. Our Santa Claus was a prolific paedophile or, in the words of the children who told me, 'a dirty old man who messed about with boys and girls and was nasty to women as well'.

Girls, their eyes wide with ghoulish excitement, told me that he had worshipped the devil. And a boy, who wanted to outdo them, described how the police had found the remains of human sacrifices on an altar in his basement. Another said there had been a whole coven of witches taking their clothes off and dancing in the moonlight before they made the sacrifices. Each story was embellished with more and more grisly details. To children this was far more exciting than anything they were allowed to read between the covers of a book.

I found out later that the gossip about human sacrifices was not true. What was true, though, was that when the police raided his home they found a room in the basement with a satanic altar. Although no human remains were found in the garden, cats that had been tortured were found hanging, dead, from the trees.

The following Saturday I was allowed to visit my family again. The capture of Uncle Ted had made the wardens treat us more carefully. In fact, during the brief time when the police were questioning some of the older children about him, our 'carers' were almost lax in their vigilance and cruelty.

CHAPTER THIRTY-ONE

Maybe it was to divert me from talking about Uncle Ted, or perhaps to stop herself picturing me sitting on the Beast of Jersey's knee, that my mother asked, for the first time, about my Christmases. For reasons understood only by the man who made the rules, the season of goodwill had to be spent at Haut de la Garenne. That was the rule, he had told my mother, when she had plucked up courage to ask.

'Not many of the children in here have parents who want them home, so it wouldn't be fair to them,' was his only explanation, my mother told me.

It made little sense as I was allowed to visit my mother on my birthday. It was not as though Colin Tilbrook cared whether any of the children got upset because one was allowed out on Christmas Day. It was doubtful that any of them would have minded. They had too many other things to deal with to give my going home much thought.

More to the point, though, was that beneath the veneer of festivities, complete with Santa handing out presents, a huge tree and a turkey dinner; lurked greed and self-interest. Haut de la Garenne's Christmas was far from happy.

What did we do, my mother wanted to know. What sort of presents had we been given? She had heard that carloads of gifts were brought to the home. She wondered why I had never talked about it, or told her what I'd received.

'It's horrible,' I told her. 'Christmas is horrible there. I hate it. I want to be here with you, Frank and Alfie.' Anger rose in me as I said my younger brother's name. 'I suppose he wakes up to a stocking full of toys,' I said, becoming tearful.

She had the grace to look embarrassed before she tried to make amends. 'But, Madeleine, you get presents from us.'

'Yes, but not on Christmas Day. I'm not with you, am I?' I screamed. Tears of rage and hurt ran down my face.

'Oh, come on,' she said, giving me a quick hug. 'Don't cry now. There must have been some good bits.' Her need to hear them was greater than my need for sympathy so I told her about helping to decorate the Christmas tree. A group of us smaller children were given the task of hanging glittering decorations on the lower branches, while the wardens and older boys climbed ladders to drape gold and silver tinsel, then pin an angel on the top. Of course we little ones wanted to go up the ladder as well. That, we were told firmly, was not allowed. They didn't want any casualties over Christmas.

The cynical side of me thinks that, as it was the one time of the year when we were under scrutiny from outside visitors, it wouldn't have looked good if children had broken bones and bruises. At any time of the day carloads of benevolent locals drew up bearing gifts for those 'in need'. Genial smiles were bestowed on us and our decorating skills were admired and praised as brightly coloured parcels were added to the growing pile under the tree.

It was not only presents for the children that were sent to Haut de la Garenne. Jersey's businessmen delivered turkeys, hams, Christmas puddings, mince pies, fruit, dates, and even boxes of crackers. Last, a huge Christmas cake decorated with imitation holly, silver balls and a tiny Santa, was carried in. In fact, they brought everything they could think of to ensure that we were all going to sit down to a feast as good as anyone else would have. They, if not the staff, were determined we would have a special day.

I'm sure for many years, when those who lived in the huge farmsteads, with high gates cut into thick walls, sat down for their Christmas dinner it warmed them to think that, thanks to them, a group of impoverished children were pulling crackers and tucking into a similar feast. They believed that the wardens had our welfare at heart and that the volunteer Santa was a kindly man who only gave out presents. When they saw us in church on Christmas morning, they no doubt imagined the delight on our faces when we returned to the home and opened our presents.

Certainly, when we marched in pairs into Gouray church for the Christmas morning service, we received kindly smiles from the congregation, especially from those who knew they had helped to improve our Christmas. Even there, though, there were certain rules, one being that the boys and girls from Haut de la Garenne had to sit on opposite sides of the church. When the collection box was passed through the congregation, we all had to put a penny into it. The coins had been given to us when, dressed in our best clothes, we had left the home for the mile-long walk.

You might be poor, but you have to learn to give as well as receive, was the message we were supposed to absorb. It certainly gained the head of the home looks of approval when we were observed doing just that.

After the service, it was back to Haut de la Garenne. Once we had changed out of our Sunday best, we made our way to the hall where the presents were shared out. There was something so impersonal about being given a parcel with 'girl 10' or 'girl 11', instead of a name on it.

When I first went to the home, Uncle Ted had handed out the gifts.

As I told my mother about those Christmases, and remembered being five and having to sit on Santa's lap, I shivered. I could still hear him asking if I had been a good girl and feel his hand stroking my knee. That was a picture I decided not to share with her. In fact, I was careful not to mention his name again. Now I knew what sort of creature he was, I wanted to block out any thoughts of him.

'What did you do with all the presents? I mean, what was it you were given? Clothes, books, toys?' my mother had asked me.

Knowing that the truth would only upset her, I toyed with the thought of telling her a few little white lies.

'Madeleine?'

The lies deserted me and the truth came out. 'We opened them. I mean, we had to because there were thank-you letters to write the next day. So we had to know what was in them.'

She looked confused. 'Well, of course you wanted to know what was in them. They were yours, weren't they?'

'I only thought that on the first Christmas,' I told her miserably remembering some of the things in the parcels I had wanted to keep. 'They went missing after that.'

'What do you mean, missing?'

'Just disappeared.'

'What – other children took them?'

'No, the wardens. You know when you came to the home and they wouldn't let you see me? You left sweets for me, didn't you?'

'Yes, I always had some with me. Just in case.'

'Well, they took them. Told me you'd left them for me. And then they just laughed when I asked for them.'

My mother was upset when she heard that. 'What reason did they give?'

'The same one they gave us when our Christmas presents disappeared.

We were naughty children and naughty children didn't deserve gifts and pretty things,' I told her.

'I used to wonder,' she said, several years later, 'why it was that when I gave you something, you always wanted to leave it at home. It wasn't because you didn't like it but because you wanted to keep it, wasn't it?'

'Yes,' I said.

CHAPTER THIRTY-TWO

There are times that stand out in our minds, not because they're bad but because they're almost perfect. Such a one was a weekend, near the end of the summer holidays, when I was eleven years old.

I was going to be allowed home, not just for one day but for three. The social worker who came to tell me the good news was younger than the ones I had met before. She dressed differently, too. Instead of a navy or grey skirt and a neat white blouse, which seemed to be the favoured outfit for those in her profession, she wore a denim skirt and a pale blue T-shirt.

Unlike the others, who, I felt, meant well but had no real idea of what it was like to be me, her face was free of makeup and her glossy dark brown hair wasn't stiff with lacquer but tied back loosely in a ponytail. 'Hello, Madeleine,' she had said, the moment I walked into the visitors' room, where she was waiting. 'I'm Michelle, a social worker.' Her dark brown eyes crinkled at the corners as she smiled.

I liked her straight away.

'Now, Madeleine,' she had said, once she had told me about my impending visit, 'I know that with your mother's asthma, walking up that hill is a bit tiring for her, so I've told her I'm going to come and collect you to save her the walk. You just be ready for ten o'clock. Make sure you pack a swimsuit. No doubt you'll be going on the beach.'

Excited, I gabbled my thanks.

She laughed. 'Oh, Madeleine, it's a pleasure. You don't need to thank me – and your mother's so looking forward to having you at home for this weekend.'

I could have hugged her just for that.

It was a Wednesday when I was given the news. 'Only two days,' I told myself, practically skipping along the corridors. And for those forty-eight hours I wore a permanent smile. I was so happy at the thought of being with my family. It was the first time I had been permitted to stay overnight since I had been returned to Haut de la Garenne.

Deep down I harboured the hope that I would be allowed to return to them. For, as children often do, I remembered only the good times – Frank humming as he cooked breakfast, my mother giving me a hug, sitting between them on the settee watching television and being allowed to stay up late at the weekend. I had pushed aside the memories of the drinking, the rows, the piles of unwashed dishes, the lack of food, and going to bed with an empty stomach. Even if I had let in the thoughts of those times when voices rose in anger, empty beer bottles littered the floor and cigarette smoke filled the air, I would still have chosen to be with them.

The excitement swelled as I allowed the seed of optimism to take root. After all, I was to spend more time than usual with them. Was that some sort of trial?

Michelle seemed so nice. She had treated me as though I was just like any other girl of my age. She acted as though it was perfectly normal for her to be arranging a visit to my mother. Surely she was the sort of person who believed that children belonged with their families.

That Friday morning I was awake before the bell announced that it was time to get up.

'Madeleine,' the warden said, when she came in to make sure we were awake, 'I hear you're going visiting this weekend.' She sounded almost friendly. My heart skipped a beat. My first thought was that she was thinking of a way to stop me. But, no: she just told me to have a bath and wash my hair. 'We want you to look your best when your taxi arrives,' she said, joking. 'Wear your Sunday outfit and, here, take these.' She handed me a pair of clean socks. 'Oh, and before you do all that, make sure your shoes are polished. Once you're ready, go and have your breakfast, then come and see me, all right?'

'What about helping clear the tables?' I asked.

'You can leave that for today. Can't having you getting your good clothes messy, can we?'

Puzzled by her attitude, but taking full advantage of it, I had my bath, dressed, put a change of clothes and a toothbrush into a bag, and I was ready.

I was late for breakfast and half expected to be told that there was none left for me but, instead, quite a generous portion was placed on my plate.

When I had finished I made my way to the warden's office. This is where there'll be a catch, I thought. They'll tell me they've changed their minds. As I knocked on the door I imagined them doubling up with laughter at my expense.

Again I was mistaken.

The warden greeted me with a smile. 'Don't you look nice?' she said, before giving me a cursory examination to make sure I had cleaned the back of my neck and that there was no dirt lurking under my nails. 'Yep, you'll do,' were her final words and I was free to go.

Clearly they wanted me neat and tidy so that I presented an image of a happy child, living in a well-run place. She had no cause for concern: my excitement at spending time with my family would have made me look as though I hadn't a care in the world.

Several minutes before ten I was hanging around in the entrance hall waiting for Michelle. As soon as I heard her Hillman Imp arrive, I rushed outside impatiently to greet her. With a grin she stepped out of the small maroon car, this time dressed in a lilac midi skirt and a lacy white blouse. That was even more different from the social-worker attire I was used to.

'Well, you look very pretty, Madeleine,' she said, placing her hand on my shoulder.

Morag Jordan had suddenly appeared and handed my bag to her. Fear gripped my tummy at the sight of her. Was she going to stop me? No, my visit must have been out of her hands. A few words were exchanged but only to discuss what time I would be returned, and then we were ready to leave.

'Have a nice time, dear,' Morag said. I looked at her in amazement, then dug my fingernails into my palms to stop myself laughing. Two-faced bitch, I thought, but, fortunately, didn't say.

No doubt Michelle believed that the smile and good wishes were genuine.

'After I deliver you, Madeleine,' she told me, 'I'm free for the rest of the day. I'm going to have a nice long walk by the beach. What about you? Any plans? Or are going to wait and see what your mother has arranged?'

'I love the beach,' I answered, 'so I hope she takes us. Then, after tea, I expect I'll be allowed to watch television.'

Seeing that I was relaxed, Michelle asked me several questions about my school, whether I'd liked it there, and was I looking forward to starting at the senior one?

I told her I didn't like lessons. 'Well, PE's all right,' I added. 'And I like drawing, but I find reading hard. The teacher gets cross and I get laughed at by the rest of the class.'

'And how do you feel about the senior school?' she asked.

'I'm scared,' I blurted out, an admission I had kept to myself until then. 'The lessons are going to be even harder, aren't they?'

Michelle didn't answer, which I took to mean yes. She gave me a brief sideways glance. 'Madeleine, if it were possible for you to go to a different school, where the lessons were not so hard, would you miss your friends?'

'What friends?' I asked. 'They all think I'm stupid because I still can't read.'

'We'll talk about that later,' Michelle told me. 'I can't tell you anything now, except that things are going to improve.'

I pestered her with questions, but she just repeated that I had nothing to worry about. 'For now, you just enjoy yourself with your family,' she told me, as we pulled up in front of the flat.

My mother must have been looking out of the window for as soon as Michelle had turned off the engine she came rushing down to greet us.

'I've just been telling Madeleine that she's not to worry about senior school,' Michelle said, and I noticed a conspiratorial look pass between them. I forgot about it the moment Michelle drove away. I had no idea then that the exchange of glances was an acknowledgement of an agreement between the two women. It would significantly change the next few years of my life.

When I went inside, every inch of the flat was gleaming. Freshly washed curtains hung at open windows, the sink sparkled, not one dirty dish or empty beer bottle was to be seen, and the floor was still damp from being mopped.

When my mother hugged me, she smelt of soap and shampoo, with only a whiff of tobacco in the mix, none of the usual alcohol fumes. 'This is going to be a proper family weekend,' she told me. 'We have some lovely things planned. Now, I know you've had breakfast, but it's never too early for cake, is it?'

Without waiting for an answer she placed a glass of orange squash and a fairy cake with pink icing in front of me. As soon as that was gone she told me to change into the pair of shorts that was on my bed. I was getting my wish: we were going to spend the day on Havre des Pas beach.

Back in the seventies, before the lido was built, that beach was a sunny south-facing strip of golden sand that was ideal for children to play on. It was also the nearest to where we lived. The blue of the sky was reflected in the sea, the smell of salt was carried on a light breeze and waves lapped gently on the shore, all conspiring to make it an idyllic summer's day. A perfect one for paddling, I thought, as we walked to our destination.

Once there, my mother, her skirt tucked up above her knees, sat with her back against a rock, a magazine in her hands and a relaxed, drowsy expression on her face. My little brother and I splashed in the shallows, then used our scooped hands as spades to make a sandcastle.

Later my mother produced sandwiches, more cake and squash, which we consumed before asking, in voices tinged with hope, if we could also have ice cream. That, we both considered, was a prerequisite for a day on the beach.

'Mustn't eat too much,' my mother told us. 'Frank's bringing fish and chips home for tea. Bless him, he knows how much you like them.' But she bought us a small cone each.

'There's another surprise for you, Madeleine,' she added, when she told us it was time to go.

'What is it?'

'Not until we're back home, so hurry up, miss!'

That made me fasten my shoes quickly.

It was not until after tea, when my brother was on the floor playing with some Lego, that I found out what the surprise was.

'Now,' Frank said, with a mischievous grin, 'what do you think we're going to do this evening?'

'Watch television?'

'No, even better! We're going to the cinema to see the latest James Bond film, *Diamonds Are Forever*. What do you think of that?'

I jumped up and down with excitement. I'd only been to the cinema on a Saturday morning, when special films were put on for children. This, I knew, was a grown-up film, one I had heard talked about at school.

'But first it's time to open your presents,' Frank said.

'Call them late birthday ones,' my mother added, going into the bedroom and coming out with two parcels.

My fingers were shaking as I untied the string and eagerly pulled off the brightly coloured paper. Inside the first was a blue cardigan and a grey pleated skirt, and in the second, a pair of soft, slip-on shoes, the ones all the girls at school wanted.

'Better try them on.' Needing no encouragement, I shot into the bedroom to change.

'You look like a proper little lady,' they said, as I preened and twirled in my new outfit.

'I think you'd better keep them on,' my mother said, before she, too, left the room to get ready.

My little brother was taken to a neighbour's house and then the three of us set off for the cinema.

I didn't know then that my visits during those summer holidays would be the last I would make to them for what was, to a child, a very long time. Neither was I aware as, munching Maltesers, I watched James Bond ousting villains and saving a beautiful girl, that certain plans had already been made for me.

CHAPTER THIRTY-THREE

Michelle had thought it better if it was my mother who broke the news that I was to leave the island. I had recently taken the 11-plus exam, as all children did in those days: it would determine what sort of secondary school we attended. That weekend I learnt that I was not grammar-school material and that the local senior school would not provide a suitable education for me. My inability to read was put down to a low level of intelligence. Because of my lack of concentration and what they viewed as occasional bouts of violence, which I saw as self-defence, I was also diagnosed with behavioural problems. No one, it seemed, had thought that depression and tiredness might have caused the first, and being bullied at school the second. I would, it was decided, benefit from being enrolled in a school that catered for children with 'special needs'.

I wish they had made up their minds about that before I'd had to sit in a room with a teacher who spoke only when the exam papers were handed out and collected. For an hour at a time I had tried to make sense of questions I could hardly read, far less answer. I had understood that everyone had to sit the 11-plus, which parents believed was important: passing or failing it would affect the rest of their children's lives. Our teachers all told us that a good education created better career opportunities. As the day of the exam approached I heard the other children telling each other the rewards they would be given if they passed: a new bike, a record player, a transistor radio were just a few. No one mentioned what would happen if they failed.

I had no such expectations. Even if my mother could have afforded such luxuries, they would not have been coming in my direction. I knew I wouldn't pass, a conviction that I'm sure my teachers shared. I wonder now why I was even made to take it. Although I'm glad I did: failing it so completely resulted in my salvation.

Frank and my mother waited until the Sunday before breaking the news that I was not to be enrolled in the local school. A new one had been found for me where, they assured me, I would be much happier. 'A school where no one will make you feel bad because you can't read,' my mother told me. 'It's a really nice place, run by nuns. Michelle showed us pictures of it and it looks perfect for you.'

She faltered then, as she tried to think of something else positive to say and Frank took over the task of explaining more about it. 'It's a special school that helps children who find learning difficult,' he said matter-of-factly. 'Everyone in your class has found ordinary school's lessons hard. So you'll all be in the same boat. And you won't get picked on any more. Means I won't have to show you how to fight any longer!' he added, laughing.

'No, you won't, Frank. Don't want her to get kicked out in her first week. Fighting is forbidden,' my mother said, giving him a reproving look. 'So don't you be putting ideas like that in her wee head!'

'You mean I won't be made to look stupid?' I asked, feeling a little glow of hope.

'No, love, you won't. And it's not true anyhow. No one's going to call you names there because you're a bit slow at some lessons,' my mother replied kindly. 'Children can be cruel, so it's a load off our minds to think you're going somewhere where bullying isn't allowed.'

This new school sounded good to me.

'Where is it?' I asked, wondering how I was going to get there each day. If I hadn't heard of it, it couldn't be near to Haut de la Garenne.

'It's in a lovely part of England,' Frank answered.

My mouth opened and formed an 'O' of shock. England was so far away: how could I go to school there? I must have looked confused because, as though reading my thoughts, Frank patted my knee reassuringly. 'It's a boarding school, which means you'll be sleeping there.'

'But when will I see you and Mum?' I asked, suddenly apprehensive.

'During the holidays, of course,' my mother answered. 'You'll only be away for the term. And from what Michelle has told us you'll be enjoying yourself so much, with all the things they do there, that time will fly by.'

'It's not all sums and reading,' said Frank, naming the two lessons I hated the most. 'They have lots of PE and dance classes – you'll love all that, right up your street.'

'And you'll be taught to cook and sew,' added my mother. 'I know you'll make plenty of new friends there. I doubt you'll miss us one little bit.'

Two different emotions were at war inside me: relief that I would be leaving Haut de la Garenne and apprehension at going into an unknown situation. Not only would I be sleeping in a strange place but I wouldn't see my family for weeks on end.

'Will you come and visit me there?'

Even though it was a question they must have been expecting, it still fell into a deep pool of silence.

'Well, love, it's very expensive for us to travel to England and we have nowhere to stay if we do. Our budget doesn't run to bed-and-breakfast places,' Frank answered eventually, flushing.

Seeing my face drop, my mother quickly enthused about the school's facilities. Not only were there no wardens, but no dormitories either. Instead there were several cottages where the children lived. 'And,' she said, 'they even have a big colour television in the lounge, which you'll be allowed to watch. Now what do you think of that?'

It sounded even better, but I understood that whatever I thought wouldn't make any difference to what happened. The decision had already been made for me by the faceless people in authority.

CHAPTER THIRTY-FOUR

2011

The worst part of being in prison was the boredom. I did not make friends with the other inmates because I knew they would want to talk about what had gone on in Haut de la Garenne, which I had no wish to share with them. Every day I walked in the exercise yard, had a cigarette there and thought about what I was going to do with my life once I got out. First, though, before I could make any changes, those demons released by the police interviews had to be exorcised.

For many reasons my chronological memory is jumbled, and I wanted my son to help me get all of my past written down in the right order: Then maybe I would find some kind of closure.

I decided I needed to see a copy of the 11-plus exam I had taken all those years ago. Failing it had changed part of my life. When my son came to visit me in the prison I asked him if he knew how I could find a copy of it.

'Sure, Mum, no problem,' he had said. 'I'll look it up on the Internet and get it printed out for you.' I doubted it would be that easy – computers were a mystery to me – but the next time he came he'd brought my exam papers with him. 'Got them,' he said, before I'd even had a chance to give him the permitted hug. 'The warden had fun looking through it all before she let you have them.' He handed me a small package of printed paper. 'I'll tell you what, though. The questions certainly aren't easy. Don't know how any kid passed that exam. Not surprised it was done away with. I mean, look at that last one, the intelligence test. Just the thing for a person who's dyslexic!'

After he had gone, I spread them out on my bed. As I looked at the maths paper, the years slipped away and I was transported back to when I'd sat in a classroom trying to decipher the questions. My hands had been so sweaty with nerves I had hardly been able to hold my pen when I wrote my name at the top of the paper. Nor did I feel any better when I saw the first question: '3755 is multiplied by 25 and the result is divided by 125. Write down the answer.' The trouble was I couldn't read it, or make sense of most of the other questions.

Panic made my stomach cramp. All I could see was a blur of jumbled squiggles. I heard the examiner telling us to put our pens down, followed by the sighs of relief from those sitting near me. When he walked down the classroom collecting our papers I waited to see what he would say when he saw that mine was not even half completed. Whatever thoughts he had he kept to himself.

We had a short break where milk was handed out. All around me comments were being made about the maths questions. Some said they were hard, others the opposite, but no one said they couldn't understand them.

The English paper was just as bad and after it came the worst: the intelligence test. 'The letters ERBDA are the letters of the word BREAD mixed up,' it told me. To a dyslexic that was what it looked like to begin with. 'Now, straighten up the following,' it commanded:

(a) AAANNB is a fruit which comes from abroad.
(b) ROHES is a large animal.
(c) GRATEAMR is a girl's name.
(d) DWEBORRA is an article of furniture.
(e) SAIRINS are used in Christmas puddings.

Every single question had been impossible for me. That day I felt such shame, such despair that, no longer caring what anyone thought, I put my head in my hands and waited for it to be over.

Michelle had fought for me to be sent to a different school from the one I had been put down for.

She understood that my inability to read had not just isolated me but also made me a target for other children's mockery.

When she arrived to collect me on the Monday morning, she came into the flat and sat down at the table, accepting my mother's offer of tea. 'Madeleine,' she said, once she had been told that I knew about the school, 'I understand that it might be a bit frightening going away from Jersey for the first time – it would be strange if it wasn't. But I want you to think about it as an adventure, which going on a plane for the first time will be. More importantly, it's a new start. Nobody at your new school is going to judge you by your lack of reading skills. You've got to believe that I wouldn't have recommended you go there if I thought they would.'

I nodded. Words were stuck behind the lump in my throat. It was the kindness more than what she was saying that had caused it.

Seeing my eyes well up, she laid her hand on mine. 'Madeleine, nobody should be made to feel ashamed if they do their best. Neither should they be told that their best is not good enough. That's why I wanted you sent to a school where the people running it will never do such a thing. Do you understand that?'

'Yes, I think so.'

'Good. Now, tell me what you do better than most of your classmates. I've been told by one of your teachers that there's something you're really good at.'

'PE,' I said, and grinned. 'I'm pretty good on the bars.'

'Now is there anything you would like to learn more of?'

I thought for a moment. 'Cooking,' I said. 'I'd like to learn to cook.'

'Then I'll let the head of your new school know that.' She chatted to my mother for a little longer, then drove me back to the home.

Just before I got out of the car, she said once more that she knew I was going to be happy at Pield Heath, which was what my new school was called.

The next few weeks passed quickly. The wardens left me alone and I was allowed to visit my family again. The day before I was due to leave, my mother arrived with an almost new suitcase. 'You'll only have to wear your school uniform on Sundays,' she said, when she handed it to me. Inside I found an assortment of clothes that Father Paul had given her the money to buy. When it came to the time for her to walk back to the bus, there were hugs, tears and more reassurances of how I was going to be happy where I was going; and then she was gone.

CHAPTER THIRTY-FIVE

The following morning Michelle drove me to the airport. There, I was handed over to an official who took me to the plane where a stewardess was waiting for me. I was shown how to fasten my seatbelt and asked if I was excited to be travelling to London, where we would arrive in less than an hour. The doors closed, and the captain informed us that the weather in London was warm and sunny. I felt us gathering speed and saw, through the tiny window, the aircraft's nose lifting and then we were in the air. As I watched Jersey disappear from view, I wondered if my mother could see the plane high in the sky above her. And if she could, would she know it was the one I was on? I had been disappointed that she wasn't at the airport to see me off. Right up to the moment when I walked on to the plane I'd hoped she would appear. Before I could become too despondent, though, the stewardess was by my side, offering me orange juice and a bag of nuts. Feeling very grown-up, I took them, leant back and let myself begin to enjoy my first ever flight.

I had hardly finished my snack when the captain was saying we were about to begin our descent. I craned my neck, trying to see what London looked like from the air. First there was a multi-coloured patchwork of fields, criss-crossed by long, winding roads, where cars, resembling Dinky or Corgi toys, drove sedately along. As we flew lower I could see rows of red-brick houses with small oblong gardens, a river and finally the airport. We're here, I thought, feeling a twinge of excitement as, with a slight bump, we landed.

The same stewardess took me to Baggage Reclaim and, once I had collected my suitcase, escorted me into the airport and handed me over to the waiting nuns. As the only other airport I had been in was the small Jersey one, the noise of Heathrow was deafening. Loudspeakers blaring, aeroplanes soaring overhead, and the babble of hundreds of people speaking different languages all combined to make me think I had landed on another planet.

The nuns must have felt the same: they led me quickly to where their car was parked. They asked, with friendly smiles, how my journey had been, and told me it would not take long to drive to the school – I would be in time for tea, they added. Then they concentrated on getting out of the airport, which left me alone to peer out of the window. Occasionally they pointed out a few features but I was too filled with excitement and nerves to take much notice.

My mind was fixed on the place where I would be spending the rest of my schooldays. What would the other children be like? Would I make friends? And how would those in charge treat me? The two who had met me from the flight seemed nice, but what if there were nuns who were no better than the wardens? Would they walk around at night shining lights into sleeping faces? My childhood experiences had taught me never to trust those who were in charge. All these doubts and questions kept surfacing, and suddenly there we were, driving into the school grounds. Stepping out of the car I was greeted by another nun, whose smile was so warm that I found my apprehension subsiding.

'Hello, Madeleine,' she said, 'welcome to Pield Heath. I'm sure you're going to be very happy here.' She drew forward a girl of about my age, with red hair and a chubby freckled face. 'Madeleine, this is Lucy,' she said, placing her hand on the girl's shoulder. 'It's her first day too. And you're both going to be staying in the same cottage.' She led us along a path to a small house. She explained that sixteen students and a nun, who in our case would be herself, lived there during term time. 'And,' she told us, with a warm smile, 'I'm a doctor, so if you're ill, you'll be in good hands.'

When we stepped inside my mouth fell open. I had never imagined it would be so warm and comfortable.

There was a group of armchairs arranged in a semi-circle, a coffee-table placed on a huge rug, and the television I had been told about, which, Sister Carmen assured us, was a colour one. There were shelves against one of the light walls, which I saw were full of jigsaw puzzles and games as well as books, and on the others hung an assortment of pictures. There was also a dining room, with several round tables, pretty bedrooms and a large shower area.

She took us outside to show us the garden, which had enough benches and seats for all sixteen girls.

Lucy and I were then shown our beds and where we could hang our clothes. As soon as we had unpacked we heard voices, which told us our housemates had arrived. 'Teatime,' said Sister Carmen, and introduced Lucy and me to the other girls. They were all friendly and curious about us, asking where we were from and what we thought of Pield Heath. A couple of them offered to take us round the grounds as soon as tea was finished and we accepted. There was a playground for when we had our school breaks, a large sports field, a vegetable garden and an orchard full of apple and pear trees. After the tour it was back to the cottage where the television was turned on for us to watch *Blue Peter*.

At dinner time, after prayers had been said, I felt as though we were a big family sitting down for a meal. Conversation was not silenced and punished but encouraged. Sister Carmen joined in and steered it so that even the shyest girl was not ignored. And the food was lovely.

Later, when I lay in my comfy bed, I knew that Michelle had been right. My life had just taken a huge turn for the better.

***

It wasn't difficult to settle into Pield Heath's routine, and within a short time it seemed like home. Every morning we assembled to say prayers followed by lessons, which were very basic. They had to be, since many of the children struggled with learning. A lot of our education was practical and hands-on, such as sewing classes with Sister Xavier. The nun in charge of helping me read used a method that no one had tried before. Instead of black print on white she said that brightly coloured letters were easier. And, amazed, I found they were. 'Don't try cursive writing,' she told me. 'It's far more difficult for you than printing.' She also used pictures with the words printed underneath so I could learn from the shapes. She made learning to read seem like a game. Under her tuition I stopped being afraid of print and gradually my reading improved.

On Saturdays there were no lessons and we were allowed to sleep in. Once we'd had breakfast we were free to explore the grounds or simply play.

'Don't we have any chores to do?' I asked Sister Carmen, the first week I was there.

'Only making your beds and tidying your rooms,' were the words that fell into my disbelieving ears.

On Sundays there were prayers and we wore our maroon uniforms to attend Mass.

My fears that the nuns might be like Haut de la Garenne's wardens were, I soon discovered, entirely groundless. They might have been strict, but they were kind. They read us books, told us stories and encouraged us to burn up our energy outside. If being allowed to sleep in at the weekend was surprising, receiving praise and hugs was even more so. Strangely, although I had craved affection, I found it hard to handle and had to stop myself cringing when an arm went around me. If they noticed, and I'm sure they did, they never commented.

There were only two things about the school that I was not comfortable with. First, I missed my family. The other girls rang home each week but I couldn't because my mother didn't have a telephone. She sent me letters, though, and with Sister Carmen's help, I managed to write back, but it wasn't the same as hearing her voice.

The second was my reaction to some of the other pupils. Some appeared to have a great deal more wrong with them than difficulty with learning. Most of the children looked like any others, but some did not and I found their appearance and behaviour frightening.

At break time, on my first school day, I noticed a couple of boys. They were so big! Not tall and muscular, but narrow-shouldered and flabby. Their lips were thick, their necks short and their heads very large in proportion to their bodies. They saw me looking at them and, to my surprise, gave me the sweetest smiles. One lumbered over until he stood just in front of me. I flinched. Was he angry that I had been staring? No! He asked my name. His voice was slower than other children's, almost slurred. When I told him I was called Madeleine, another beautiful smile lit his face.

'That's pretty,' he said, and I relaxed. I asked him what he was called and he told me he was David and his friend was Sam. I decided then that, whatever he looked like, he was all right.

The girl in the wheelchair, who sat staring at nothing, disturbed me more. I wanted to turn my eyes away, but I couldn't. I was fascinated by her, especially as she kept emitting a cry followed by disjointed mumbling. Then she began to rock backwards and forwards, so violently that I wondered if she might turn the chair over.

A nun came over and sat nearby but not too close to her. I couldn't hear what she was saying but I imagined it was something soft and soothing as gradually the rocking ceased.

There were others, too. One boy made no eye contact with anyone as he silently sorted his food into different colours before he could eat his lunch, and another had to have everything cut into the smallest pieces. The one who disturbed me most was a boy of about my age, who, in the classroom, suddenly threw a tantrum, much like my little brother used to do. The difference was that Alfie had been a toddler when he did it.

What was the matter with these kids? That question was quickly followed by another. *Do they think there's something wrong with me too? Is that why I've been sent here?*

It was Sister Carmen who put my mind at rest. 'Madeleine,' she said, when I was sitting in her office one day, 'was it explained to you what we try to achieve here?'

I thought carefully before I replied. 'You help children who find learning difficult.'

'Yes, that's right. But we also help some who have other problems.'

Yes, I thought, like acting really strangely!

'Not everyone is the same,' said Sister Carmen softly, as though reading my thoughts. 'This is a special school for special people who need our help and guidance.'

'But what's wrong with the girl in the wheelchair?' I asked. 'Why was she rocking like that?'

'She cannot find words easily, so if she is distressed, she communicates that to us by rocking. Then there are pupils like the boy you were talking to earlier. He and his friend both find lessons very difficult, much more than you do. We teach them what are called social skills, too, as well as how to look after themselves. Our aim is to make sure that when they leave here they can be independent. We also have children who come for a short time so their parents can have a holiday or just get a bit of rest. The girl in the wheelchair is one. Those children need a lot of care.'

'Will she ever get better?' I asked.

'If you mean, will she ever walk and be able to live alone, then the answer is no. Now I want you to understand that there will be occasions when you will see behaviour that you may find . . . let's say odd. You don't have to understand why it is. That is what we are here for. What you mustn't be is frightened of it or unkind to the person because they are different. Now do you have any questions?'

'Well, Sister Carmen, that boy who lost it in class, what was that all about?'

'Jason, you mean. He's one of our brightest students. I see you look surprised. Let me try to explain what one of his problems is. You thought he had a tantrum but he didn't. He doesn't get really angry, just frustrated. One has to be able to read his mind or his body language to know if he's about to break. We try as hard as we can not to let it happen. Think about your last school, when you couldn't do something right, no matter how often you were shown. How did you feel?'

'Cross with myself,' I answered.

'Well, that's how he feels sometimes. Not because he can't read, but because he doesn't know how to improvise. Now let me ask you a question, if a door was jammed and beside you there was a screwdriver, what would you do?'

That was easy. I had seen Frank use one when a window had stuck.

'Pick it up and wriggle it around where the catch is,' I said promptly.

'Good. That is what you would do, but Jason couldn't. You see, for him a screwdriver is for screws. But a jemmy is used for prising things open. So if he can't find the right tool for the job, he simply won't be able to do the task. Then he gets frustrated. Now let me ask you something else, Madeleine. How did you feel when you had to take those tests?'

'Bad,' I answered.

'Hopeless?'

'Yes.'

'So already you know a little more about how he feels, Madeleine,' she said, with a smile. 'During the time you are here I know you will learn not to judge people by how they look or, indeed, how they act. You have to see past that to what is important. Just remember that a kind soul is a beautiful one.

'Now let's talk about you for a moment. I know you have had problems with reading. That is something we're working on with you. We're trying to make it easier for you. Are you enjoying it?'

'Yes,' I answered. 'I mean, I do get upset about not being able to read, and,' I blurted, 'they used to laugh at me and I hated it.' That was the first time I'd been able to admit how I'd felt.

'No one will laugh at you here, I promise you that. Now maybe you can see why you have been sent here. Just as Jason needs a different input from what mainstream or ordinary schools provide, children who find some lessons difficult do as well. Now do you understand what it is we do here?'

'Yes, Sister Carmen, I do.'

She placed her arms around me and gave me a hug, and for that brief moment, I felt something I hadn't experienced since I'd left the crèche: safe.

Sister Carmen was right. My reading improved, my confidence grew, I learnt to see past physical appearances and, for the first time in many years, I trusted those in charge of me.

Half-term came and went. That holiday, I stayed at the school. Then the next one came, and I returned to Jersey for the Christmas holidays.

CHAPTER THIRTY-SIX

2011

I was aware of Morag Jordan watching me almost as much as I had studied her during my first few days in prison. Was she puzzled by my calmness? Wondering if I was just biding my time? Did she expect me to approach her and issue threats?

I doubt she would have understood that she was no longer important to me. I believed, since my son had told me about the coverage of the Jordans' case on the internet, that her real punishment would come when she was released. No one enjoys being vilified and that was what was happening. Would she be aware when she was handed her possessions as she readied herself to walk free that reporters would be camping out waiting for her to appear? Did she suspect that the moment those heavy prison gates swung open she would be deafened by shouted questions and blinded by the flash of cameras and the penetrating glare of TV lights? And while she stood outside, disoriented by the noise around her, those victims from forty years ago, whom she had abused and humiliated, would be yelling their hatred. I took comfort in imagining the now notorious couple being recognised wherever they went. Fingers would be pointed and faces would be hostile. For them there would be no more slipping down to the local pub or shopping where once they had been greeted warmly.

There was a memory I wanted to push back into the oblivion but it refused to be ignored: my return to Haut de la Garenne after my first term at the special school. Just letting it surface brings back all the misery I felt then.

On the flight to Jersey I had been so excited. I was going to see my mother after all these weeks and I had so much to tell her. I was impatient to arrive in Jersey. Would she be waiting for me? I was sure she would and, grabbing my case from the baggage carousel, I practically ran through the airport. I looked about expectantly – and saw Michelle.

'Where's my mother?' I asked.

She looked uncomfortable. 'You'll see her very soon,' she said. 'She's going to visit you tomorrow.'

'Visit me? Why aren't I staying with her?' I didn't wait for her response because it was my next question that I really wanted the answer to. 'So where am I going?' I asked, although I was dreading the answer.

'To Haut de la Garenne, of course.'

I pleaded with her not to take me there. By the time it took us to reach her car, my face was wet with tears.

'Madeleine, it's not up to me,' she said, as soon as I was in the passenger seat. 'There's nothing I can do. You were made a ward of court when you were almost killed that time. It was all explained to you. I know you love your mother and she loves you, but she just cannot cope. Haut de la Garenne is considered safer for you. It's your wellbeing that we're thinking of, you know that.'

Why, oh, why did I not say anything then? It was the opportunity to tell her what was happening in that vast grey building, and that the very man trusted to look after me was a monster.

However difficult it was to find the words, I should have told her about the sexual acts Colin Tilbrook had forced me to perform ever since I was five. Even after he left, when I was eleven, his influence remained in the brutality of the Jordans and the blind eyes turned when staff sexually abused children. If only I had spoken out, imagine the difference it would have made – not just to me but to many others. For Tilbrook continued to work in children's homes after his departure from Haut de la Garenne.

After years of guilt, I have finally come to understand why children rarely talk. I, like so many abused children, had been told that if I did tell, very bad things would happen to me. I would not be believed, and even if I was I, too, would be blamed. Colin Tilbrook had manipulated me to such an extent that I had become complicit in hiding the abuse. I had smiled at him in public, said, 'Yes, sir', 'please' and 'thank you', and never showed either my fear or my hatred. By the age of eleven I felt as though I was also guilty. I had kept that secret for almost as long as I could remember. It was shaming and the fear of reprisals stopped the words tumbling out. Instead I tightened my lips, forced the tears to stop and said nothing.

Thinking that my silence showed I accepted the arrangement, Michelle told me she had some good news. I was going to spend Boxing Day with my family. 'I did ask Mr Tilbrook if you could spend Christmas with them, too,' she told me, 'but, as you know, he's very strict about that. He wants everyone to stay together. But I managed to persuade him to let you go the next day. So, cheer up, it's not far off. Now I want to hear all about the new school. I've had a letter from Sister Carmen, who speaks very highly of you. She says you've settled in very well and are working hard.'

I managed to tell her how much I liked it there and that I enjoyed the reading lessons.

'That's good, Madeleine, and after only one term!'

'They make them fun,' I said.

I might have been making the right sounds, but my stomach was churning. I knew what was waiting for me. Michelle did not.

Colin Tilbrook sent a boy to fetch me on the first night.

With every step I took down the corridor, I pictured what was going to happen once I was in that gloomy office. Reaching it, the boy raised his hand and knocked once. Colin Tilbrook's voice bade us come in.

'Hello, Madeleine,' said the man I feared and hated. He dismissed the messenger and I was left standing by his desk.

He smiled and my knees shook. His expression told me that whatever he had planned was going to be worse than anything he had done before.

'Well, Madeleine, flying to London all by yourself! Quite the little sophisticate, aren't you? Eleven already, almost a teenager. Now, I suppose you're well versed in the facts of life. You'll know about babies and where they come from. The nuns have taught you all that, I expect?'

'Yes,' I muttered. Although I could have said that I was pretty well versed before I'd gone.

'Have you started your periods yet?'

My face burnt. I thought he was just trying to embarrass me. It took me a few years to understand the real reason he'd asked.

Colin Tilbrook did not like the girls in his care becoming pregnant. Too many questions might be asked. When it had happened, as it did occasionally, the girl involved had been quickly sent away. But I was a ward of court and could not be made to disappear. Now I was a little older he had decided that the type of sex a five-year-old was capable of participating in could be made a whole lot more interesting.

That evening he raped me. I put up a fight, a pitiful one that I had no chance of winning. I knew what he wanted from the moment he drew the curtains, locked the door and told me to undress. I knew he was going to hurt me. Even worse than the pain he would inflict was the thought of that part of his body pushing inside me. There was no cushion or pillow for him to pick up so instead he spread his hand, which stank of stale cigarettes, over my mouth.

'Stop struggling, Madeleine,' he hissed, and pushed me against the desk until my shoulders were almost touching it. I tried to bite those thick fingers. I wanted to draw blood. He laughed, then lifted my head and banged it down. Not hard enough to render me unconscious, that would have spoilt his fun, but hard enough to bring tears of fear to my eyes.

My underclothes were swiftly pulled down, my legs spread apart by his knees and he was inside me. With every thrust, he hurt me so much that I felt I was being torn in two. My whimpers of pain only excited him. His breath grew louder, his thrusts harder, his body shook and his weight collapsed against me. For a moment I was pinned there. Then, with a satisfied grunt, he stood up.

Nausea welled and I swallowed the acrid taste. I didn't want to throw up in front of him again. I didn't want to cry either. But I did.

'I'm going to tell, I am,' I sobbed, after he had turned his back to me.

He laughed again. 'Really, Madeleine? You think anyone will believe a little girl like you? You're so stupid that you can't even go to a normal school on the island, can you? And who do you mix with in your new school, eh? Retards, that's who.'

I wanted to scream that he was lying: my school was for special children. I had made friends there and I was happier than I had ever been, but the tears that streamed from my eyes and ran down my nose blocked my throat.

Unmoved by a little girl, who was almost incoherent with shock, he continued talking. 'As for those nuns I hear you've grown fond of, do you really think they'd like you if they found out about all the mortal sins you've been committing? They wouldn't even let you stay at the school Madeleine. Not with all your impure thoughts. Then where would you be? Back here, that's where. Here, where no school wants you either.'

Through my misery and pain his words sank in. I believed every one of them and he knew it. And, knowing he had won, his voice became friendlier. 'Come, Madeleine, it's not too bad. You'll grow to like it. It always hurts the first time. I'm going to give you something to make you feel better.' He put a glass of amber liquid into my hand. 'When you leave here there'll be plenty of boys after you,' he told me, as pain shot into my stomach and blood dribbled down my legs. 'Now drink that up.'

Shakily, I put the glass to my lips, smelt something strong and hesitated.

'Swallow it,' he ordered. I took a big gulp and he was right: the warm sensation made me feel calmer, if not better.

'A little brandy and cola does the trick, all right.' He took the glass and poured more into it.

The room begun to spin and, as if from far away, I heard him telling me that my mother was coming the next day. 'You want to see her, don't you?'

'Yes,' I answered.

'Well, behave, Madeleine, that's all I am asking you to do. No more silly-little-girl threats. Understand?'

I understood. 'Yes,' I replied.

'Yes what, Madeleine?'

'Yes, sir.'

CHAPTER THIRTY-SEVEN

At night, Colin Tilbrook crawls into my dreams. Lying on my prison cell's narrow bed, I see the silhouette of his dark, bulky frame, carrying a pillow. A pulse of fear lodges in my throat. He's in my room, inching closer and closer, until he's hovering just above me. His breath is on my skin, rank and sour. I try to scream but only a groan escapes me. Then I'm awake, my heart racing, my hair wet with sweat. I'm too frightened to go back to sleep. Is it close proximity to Morag Jordan that causes these nightmares? I don't want to return to that dream. If I do, I'll hear his voice, the mocking tones I recall so well, and feel his hands crawling over my body that is suddenly young again. The air in my cell feels thin, my throat tight, as I lie there, fists clenched, waiting for the fear to fade. I welcome the harsh shrill of the bell telling me it's time to get up. I hear the warden's footsteps, my door is unlocked and, groggy, I go for breakfast. Tilbrook will return, along with the other ghosts of my childhood, unless I confront my past, look at it one more time and make peace with it, before returning the images to the box labelled 'dealt with' where they belong.

I know I have blocked out some of what happened to me. That, I have been told, is the subconscious mind's way of protecting me from memories that are too painful to cope with. But if that is the case why can I recall so sharply the years until I was eleven? It is only when I try to travel back to the later years that my recollections become so fuzzy that they seem almost unreal. What happened over the remainder of that Christmas holiday? My head aches with the attempt to remember. There was snow, thick sheets of it, that I had to run through, and a small artificial tree decorated with glittering lights in a corner of my mother's tiny flat. I was given presents, but I cannot picture what they were. I make myself concentrate until a small segment of that time unfolded.

It was night. Outside the windows there was only darkness. A torch was shining, its light blinding me. Behind the glow there were shadowy figures. I could hear whispers, stifled laughter. Hands grabbed my arms and pulled me out of bed. Other girls were receiving the same treatment and our fear hung in the air, taking away our ability to speak. Instead we stood in the middle of the dormitory, shivering with fear and cold. 'Party time, girls,' the voices behind the torches said.

Holding an arm or shoulder, they took us to the stairs leading down to the cellars. Still none of us uttered a word, not even to ask what they wanted. Drink had made them jolly, but that, we were aware, could change to belligerence in seconds. Asking questions had too often resulted in a fist or foot lashing out. We were powerless to do anything but go along with what they wanted and hope it wouldn't take them too long to become bored with us; we were their toys.

Down there, in those low-ceilinged rooms, we could hear men's and women's voices. Music was playing, harsh, thumping sounds that added to my intense feeling of dread. 'Swallow this, Madeleine. It'll make you feel good,' a voice said. A tablet was slipped between my lips and my chin held upwards until it had gone down my throat. We moved along the passageway to the room where the music was coming from. I felt as though I was floating. Through the flickering candlelight I looked down upon figures writhing on a pile of cushions, and over the music I could hear the laughter and groans of the almost naked men and women who were touching, rubbing and grasping each other. The taste of my first cigarette comes to me, as does the memory of my choking. Hands stroked me, voices told me I was pretty, my pyjama top was unbuttoned and hands touched my still flat chest, before fingers went under the elastic of the bottoms. Then . . . nothing.

I woke up hours later in my bed. My head throbbed and my body felt sore. My mind, my adult self realised, had not blocked out what had taken place: the pill had. Was it during those holidays that I saw the boy in the shower? He was the second who had killed himself. I know I was still very young. A girl, almost hyperventilating with shock, came running into the common room screaming that there was a dead boy in the showers. Before we could be stopped, we all swarmed in. Like the boy in the tree, he had hanged himself.

I tried to focus on his feet, which were still moving, but almost imperceptibly, like the pendulum of a clock that has stopped ticking. I didn't look up – I couldn't bear to confront those dead eyes – so I only saw him from the waist down. He was wearing grey trousers.

I knew who he was. He and his sister had arrived at the home just a few weeks earlier. I felt very sorry for them when I heard they had been brought there because their mother was too ill to look after them. It was their closeness to each other that made me notice them. He was about ten, a slight boy, who clung to his sister while she, no more than twelve, would stand with her arm around him, talking softly to him. Over the short time they were in the home they appeared to be inseparable. But not inseparable enough, it seems, to protect him from predators.

I don't know what happened to her. I never saw her after that day. What I did know, though, was the almost inevitable fate of pretty boys. And he was certainly that. If he had lived, he would have grown into a very handsome man, with lots of floppy blond hair and big sad eyes. Like other pretty boys, before and after, he had been taken to Victoria Tower, an ancient circular building with a staircase connecting its three small rooms. Surrounded by tree-filled slopes and overlooking the castle and Anne Port Bay, it is a beautiful place. But there was no beauty in the terrible acts that went on there.

A male warden raped him. Three of us, seeing him being led off, had followed them. From outside the building we heard the boy's desperate cries, then a long agonised scream and knew instinctively what had happened. We knew there was nothing we could do to intervene so, guiltily, we left our hiding place and returned silently to the common room.

He escaped from Haut de la Garenne the only way he knew how: by climbing on to a chair, tying one end of a sheet around his neck and the other round the shower rail.

I cried for him that night as did the other two girls who had been with me when we had followed them. We shared his secret and our guilt.

CHAPTER THIRTY-EIGHT

Did Colin Tilbrook send for me again? He must have, but there's a merciful blank where that particular memory should be, as is my journey back to school. However, when I close my eyes, the nightmares I had over that term slip into my mind. They still plague me. They woke Sister Carmen, who hurried into my room. 'Just a bad dream, Madeleine,' she told me soothingly, and sat with me until I fell asleep.

'Did you watch television and see some horror movies you shouldn't?' she asked. That was how she explained my bad dreams and I didn't correct her. Gradually they diminished, then ceased: nothing bad would happen at that school. No one was going to pull me out of bed and march me away.

As the Easter holidays approached, the other girls chattered about their forthcoming holiday. Maybe they'll think it's too short to send me back to Jersey, I speculated hopefully.

No, they did not.

Michelle was waiting for me when I arrived. 'Good news,' she told me, with a huge smile. 'I've arranged for you to spend this holiday at La Preference. Madeleine, it's a really great place. I know some of the staff there and they make sure that holiday time is fun. It's not nearly as big as Haut de la Garenne, so it's nice and cosy. And there are lots of things to do there.'

She was right. It was even better than she had described. There were bikes that groups of us could explore the countryside on, a record player, music, books and a big assortment of toys and games. There were even several copies of the popular girls' magazine, *Jackie*. Every day was different and interesting: the staff encouraged us to go outside unless it rained and then board games and jigsaw puzzles were brought out. My mother was even given tea and was made welcome when she came to La Preference to see me, and I was given permission several times to visit her. This time the days went far too quickly.

It was not until Michelle collected me at the end of the holiday that she told me she was leaving Jersey for good the following month. She wouldn't be there when I returned for my summer holidays. She reassured me that she would write and told me she wanted to hear that I was continuing to do well at school. But, however hard she tried, I felt abandoned. Out of all the people in authority I had encountered, she was the only

CHAPTER THIRTY-NINE

The long summer holidays arrived. Although I wished I was staying with my mother, I was looking forward to spending time at La Preference. Even though the Easter holiday had been short, I had made some friends. I glanced around the plane at the other passengers. Although there were several teenagers who, I presumed, were also returning to Jersey for the holidays, as usual I was the only one travelling alone. There was a little group of girls, slightly older than me; from the snippets of their conversation I overheard, I gathered that they were all at the same boarding-school and were excited at the prospects of a fun-filled holiday. On the short flight, I looked forward to seeing my family and thought of all the things I wanted to do once I was back at La Preference.

I had asked whether my mother could meet me at the airport and take me to La Preference but Sister Carmen had informed me that I had to be accompanied by a social worker: it was a court requirement. I was met by a woman of stocky build, somewhere in her thirties. She gave me her social-worker smile, as her eyes examined me, and introduced herself as Mrs Henry.

I saw the group of girls from the plane rushing towards their parents with cries of excitement, straight into welcoming arms. I could only guess what they were being told as they were hugged and kissed, how well they looked, how much they had been missed and then assurances that lots had been planned for them to do. Oh, how I wanted the same warm welcome. I wanted it so badly it hurt.

'Well, Madeleine, are you pleased to be back in Jersey?' she asked, breaking into my daydream. I nodded, already missing the friendly, easy-going Michelle who, with her generous smile, always made me feel she was genuinely happy to spend time with me.

'I've spoken to your mother,' she told me, as she led the way to her car. 'She can't wait to visit you.' I couldn't think of anything to say to that, for I knew my mother missed me. 'And I expect you're looking forward to seeing her too?' she probed. I nodded and she, ignoring my lack of response, carried on with her almost scripted questioning.

A few more standard items about school, making friends and the lessons I liked most, then her efforts dried up. Now I could relax.

I was lost in another daydream of being with my mother on the beach, our faces turned up to the sun, so I didn't notice straight away that we were on the wrong road. 'This isn't the way to La Preference,' I said, feeling my first flicker of unease.

'Oh, were you not told?' She knew the answer to that question as well as I did.

'Told what?'

'We have had to make different arrangements for you. There wasn't any room there, so we arranged for you to stay somewhere just as suitable.'

'So where are you taking me?' I asked, feeling as though a stone had lodged in my stomach.

'You're to spend this holiday at Haut de la Garenne.'

The effect of hearing that name was immediate. My heart pounded and my hands became clammy with sweat. I pressed myself back in the seat. 'No.' I'm sure she had been told how I would react and had wanted to reach the home before I realised where I was being taken.

I knew that nothing would make her turn the car around and drive in the direction I wanted to go but that didn't stop me protesting. I didn't want to sound like a petulant child but the words refused to stay inside me. In a continuous babble I said I hated Haut de la Garenne, it wasn't fair that I was being taken there, why could I not be with my mother, and if Michelle was still in Jersey this would not be happening. It all fell on what seemed to me to be disinterested ears. She didn't think to question why a child who had appeared normal, if quiet, on her arrival at the airport had become almost hysterical at hearing the name Haut de la Garenne.

She told me to stop being a silly little girl: she had more important things to do than listen to my irrational nonsense. I tried once more and this time she became angry. 'Madeleine, if you don't stop this right now I'll have to report you when we arrive. Now,' her voice softened slightly, 'I don't want to have to do that. Not on your first day back.'

I forced myself to be both quiet and still, but my mind was working furiously. Let her believe the threat's worked, I thought, as a little voice in my head whispered, 'Escape, Madeleine.'

I told her I was sorry. I needed to make her relax. At the same time I surreptitiously released the catch on my seatbelt. She neither noticed my fingers pressing it nor that I was watching the traffic lights. They had changed to amber and she, like the drivers in front of us, was slowing to a crawl. I opened the door and, before she could grab me, my feet were on the ground. She was shouting angrily, demanding I get back into the car 'right now' as though that would make me change my mind.

'Screw that for a laugh,' I said to myself, as, giggling, I took off. She couldn't leave her car at the traffic lights with other vehicles behind her. There was nothing she could do until she was able to pull over and park. As my feet pounded along the pavement I ignored the stitch in my side, turned down a side-street and kept going.

Nothing was going to stop me. I didn't think in those first few minutes about where I could go to hide from the authorities or ask myself what they would do to me when they found me. That was not something I was prepared to face. All I could think was that I was free and that I had finally cocked a snook at those who ruled my life.

Going straight to my mother's was out of the question. Her flat would be the first place they looked for me. The moment the police were informed that I had run away, a patrol car with a couple of burly policemen inside would be dispatched to pay her a visit. For the first time I felt a pang of remorse. No doubt whoever was sent would act as though they didn't believe a word she said. They would practically accuse her of lying and insist on looking in every room. I thought of her distress, not just because I was missing but because of the sneers she would see on their faces.

The adventure was already beginning to pall.

In the end I went to one of my mother's friends.

'There'll be trouble all right,' she said, when I told her what I had done. 'Still, you might as well make the best of it before they find you.'

She agreed to pop round to my mother's flat, as she put it, to make sure the coast was clear. 'But not until the police have been and gone,' she said sensibly. 'You don't want to get your mum into any trouble, do you?'

It was dark when, under cover of the shadows, I made my way to the small block of flats where my mother lived.

'Oh, Madeleine darling, what have you done? The police have been here looking for you,' she exclaimed, the moment she saw me. 'They told us that if you turned up here we had to get in touch straight away. That if we let you stay, we'd be charged. The cheek of it, saying I'd be in trouble for spending time with my own daughter,' she added indignantly.

'I've run away. I don't want to go back to Haut de la Garenne. I just can't, Mum.'

'I know you hate it there, love. But what choice is there? It's only for a few weeks, and then you'll be back at that nice school. You don't want that spoilt now, do you? You're happy there.'

'You know she's right, Madeleine,' said a worried Frank. 'You'll have to go back. There'll be a load of trouble for us, too, if you don't. Better if you do it yourself and not wait for them to find you. Look, I'll come with you, if you like. I can take you to the children's office, not the police. Then you say you're sorry and they'll take you to Haut de la Garenne. It's the only solution, Madeleine.'

I knew he was right. I could see from the worried look on my mother's face that she was scared of the repercussions if I was caught at the flat.

'If they think I put you up to it, they might stop us seeing you,' she said.

The fight went out of me when I saw tears were not far away. They were right, of course: until I was back in the home the police would keep coming back to my mother's flat, for Jersey was a tiny place. 'Can I have something to eat first?' I asked.

'And then we'll go to the children's office,' Frank said.

'No, I'll go. You don't need to come with me,' I said firmly, suddenly understanding that they, too, were scared of the authorities. I had heard my mother curse them, but I had not understood that she was frightened of the police and the social workers. Maybe she believed that one mistake would cost her Alfie as well as all her other children.

'If I go on my own, it will look as though you never saw me,' I said.

He hugged me, and that expression of gratitude warmed me.

A worn frying pan was placed on the stove, a generous slice of butter melted and then in went a slice of bread, two eggs and a thick rasher of streaky bacon. In no time I was tucking into what we called an Irish fry. The only things missing were black pudding and laughter.

I knew there was trouble ahead for me and so did they.

As soon as I had swallowed the last mouthful I left. In my pocket I had the coins Frank had given me to make a phone call and a scrap of paper with the children's office's number on it.

I never got to the phone box: I was spotted by a police car and taken to the station. Two members of staff came for me: Morag and Anthony Jordan. I was thrown into the back of the car, and Morag climbed in beside me. 'I wouldn't try to get away from me. Anthony might just run you over when we chase you.' She laughed.

Once we were through the home's doors they picked me up by the arms, dragged me down those stairs and threw me into the detention cells. I screamed and kicked. I tried to place my feet against the wall to prevent them dragging me but, however hard I struggled, it was no good. Mercifully they didn't strip me that time but there was no blanket and, although it was a summer evening, I was instantly cold. They turned off the lights and I was left in the dark, huddled in the corner furthest from the door.

CHAPTER FORTY

The door swung open, letting in light. Thinking I was going to have my clothes stripped off, I wrapped my arms round my body and stayed huddled in the corner with my head down. 'It's all right, Madeleine.' Through my terror I heard Anne's voice for the first time. She was saying she had been sent to fetch me and that everything was going to be all right. Even then I recognised something in her voice that told me she would not turn into a sadistic bully like the majority of her workmates. 'I'm going to take you to get your breakfast.'

Glancing up, I saw a round-faced young woman whose soft, coffee-brown eyes gazed compassionately at me. She took my hand, wrapped warm fingers around mine and pulled me gently to my feet. 'Come,' she said, and led me out of the cell.

Once we had climbed the short flight of steps that led us back into the main part of the building, she told me she had been asked to talk to me.

'What about?' I asked suspiciously. Wardens did not as a rule have conversations with us. They shouted instructions and meted out punishments.

'One of the children's officers is coming to see you later today. Before she does, we want to see if we can come up with some sort of plan to stop you being so unhappy here. Mrs Henry evidently reported that it was only when you heard you were coming here that you became hysterical. She said you seemed so excited to be back until that point.'

I looked at her incredulously. Did she not know what went on at Haut de la Garenne? Or why no child in their right mind would want to be returned there?

'Do you think she might have me moved?' I asked hopefully, ignoring what she had said about a plan to make me happier. Not being there would certainly see to that.

'No, Madeleine. But she might write in her file that your behaviour is that of a delinquent. I assure you that is definitely something you don't want on your record. You've been here off and on for a long time. And there is nothing in any of the social worker's notes saying that you have complained of being treated badly. I doubt you can shift the blame for what you did on to the home. I know there have been problems here. But I'm not the only member of staff who is new. Colin Tilbrook has been replaced as well.'

A huge wave of relief swept over me. But he was not the only one who had abused me. As I thought this through, I eyed her with suspicion and wondered if she was just warning me that whatever I told the children's officer would not be believed. Should I tell them what had happened, not just to me but to other children as well? Maybe I'd be accused of making up disgusting stories. I shivered. Perhaps Anne had no idea of the cruelty and abuse that had driven at least two desperate children to kill themselves.

'Anyhow,' she continued, 'first, go to the dining hall and get something to eat. We'll have a chat afterwards.' She gave me a light push in the direction of the doors, then walked away.

Anne made sure that she and I had our talk. When I finished my breakfast I found her waiting for me. We went to one of the staffrooms where, instead of being made to stand while I was told how bad my behaviour was, she motioned for me to sit opposite her. Instead of the expected lecture she asked a question, which as far as I could see, had little bearing on the reason I was there.

'Do you know the story of Geoffrey's Leap?'

I shook my head, confused.

'Long ago,' she told me, 'a man known only as Geoffrey committed a heinous crime. One that was punishable by death. Not by hanging – that was for lesser sins. Geoffrey's crime was so bad that it was decided he would be thrown from the highest point on the island into the sea.

'Now,' Anne continued when she saw she had gained my attention, 'he could have run away, as other men might have done. There is a narrow strip leading from behind the church to the beach named the Sanctuary Path and that was considered sacred land. Once he stepped on to it he would be safe, for no one would have dared arrest him there. His friends, or so the story goes, urged him to take it. They would have a boat waiting to sail across the sixteen miles to France. But Geoffrey was a rather cocky young man. Instead of fleeing, he decided to challenge the executioner. He would survive, he said.'

'And did he?'

'Wait, Madeleine,' she said firmly. 'Just pay attention to the story. The crowds gathered. Watching the throwing of a man to his death was considered good entertainment then. Two burly guards escorted Geoffrey up to the top of the peak, where he was handed over to the executioner, a mountain of a man, who hid his identity behind a leather mask.

'The crowd roared their approval when the masked man picked up Geoffrey, as easily as though he weighed no more than a child, lifted him high into the air and hurled him headlong over the edge towards the rocks and the sea so far below. Much to the crowd's amazement, and I'm sure the executioner's too, Geoffrey did what no man before him had done. He stretched his arms out, made a perfect dive into the sea, then swam triumphantly ashore. The crowd went berserk. The executioner had not done his job properly, they shouted. Geoffrey must be thrown in again.

'Although many called for the punishment to be repeated others, mainly women, for he was a very good-looking man, shouted that he deserved to live. He had been given the punishment the law decreed, and if Death had not wished to take him he should go free.

'Now, as I said, Geoffrey was a cocky young man. He strutted and preened in front of the crowd, relishing the women's admiration and being the centre of attention. Turning to his audience he said he would settle the argument. The executioner could throw him into the sea again.'

'And?' I asked impatient to hear the ending.

'He drowned. There was no reprieve the second time.'

Later, when I learnt that the heinous crime was the raping of a young maiden I thought he had deserved his fate, but the first time I heard the tale I felt a bit sorry for him.

'Just goes to show that pride comes before a fall, Madeleine,' said Anne, to which I made no reply. I knew there had to be a reason for her telling me the story and I waited to hear what it was.

'Now,' she said cheerfully, 'the good thing to come out of that incident is that three hundred years later the rock, which is named after Geoffrey, has become a major tourist attraction. There is nothing our summer visitors like more than hearing the story of how he drowned the second time. Now, what do tourists want after they have listened to a bit of ghoulish Jersey folklore, climbed up the rocks and sunbathed for a bit?'

Before I could say I didn't know, she answered for me. 'Tea, of course! Especially our English visitors. I'm not sure about the French.'

I still couldn't see what this had to do with me, but as anything was better than being scolded for impertinence, I didn't interrupt her.

'Now, Madeleine,' she said, with an impish grin, 'don't look so puzzled. I'm getting to the bit I think you're going to like. So be patient for just a little while longer, all right?'

I nodded and she continued: 'There's a couple I know who own a tea shop near those famous rocks. I've spoken to them about you and they've agreed to give you a part-time job over the holidays. It means you'll be earning your own money. That will be a good thing, won't it? You need some new clothes and wouldn't it be nice to be able to choose them and pay for them yourself?'

I could hardly believe my ears. Would I like to earn money of my own? Oh, yes, I certainly would. It seemed too good to be true.

'And,' Anne continued, 'it means you won't be in here all the time. Of course you'll still be able to visit your mother, as long as you give me your word that there will be no more running away. Shall I tell the tea shop you'd like to work there?'

'Yes, oh, yes, please, miss,' I gasped.

'And will you promise that if I do this for you there'll be no more running away?'

'I won't run away again, I swear,' I said.

'Good. I trust you not to let me down. And tomorrow when the social worker comes, you'll just say you wanted to see your mother so much that you just took off. I think that's the best explanation, don't you?'

I recognised, when it was spelt out like that, exactly what the deal was. If I didn't complain about the staff in the home, they would make my life easier, for the moment anyway.

'All right,' I said.

CHAPTER FORTY-ONE

The next day I started work in the tea shop. Just two hours over lunchtime and more on a Saturday, I was told. The place was packed with good-natured tourists.

'A bit young, aren't you?' one or two said.

'I'm working for the school holidays to buy new clothes,' I told them. Magic words when it came to the size of my tips. Coins and even the odd ten-shilling note were dropped into the tip jar. At the end of the week my share was handed to me. It was more money than I had ever held in my hands before.

I asked Anne to come with me to help me choose a new dress. I tried on one after another and finally settled on a pretty blue full-skirted one with a square neckline trimmed with white. I felt so proud when I took my own money out to pay for it. Afterwards we went and had tea in one of the many cafés that had opened in the centre of town.

Once we were there I stopped seeing her as a warden but more as someone who had gone out of her way to help me. Why? I wondered again. When I asked her, she looked at me knowingly. 'There have been a few changes in the home,' she said. 'I think things are better now. Not quite so strict. So I thought it better if you told the social workers you wouldn't run away again and that you were sorry. And you are happier there now, aren't you?

If I didn't fully understand then, I do now. Perhaps when she had spelt out the deal she had engineered for me, Anne knew if I talked I would not be believed. She might not have known the extent of the abuse that had taken place in the home, but she certainly knew some had. She could have learnt that from talking to the children and observing them. But without proof she would have been a lone voice if she had reported any suspicions to the authorities. She was only at the home for a year and during that time the physical abuse lessened to some extent. Like Michelle's, her departure left a gap in my life.

The rest of that summer holiday passed uneventfully. Not that I ever grew to trust the wardens. And although I still hated being at Haut de la Garenne, I was allowed to visit my mother, save some money, and the couple who owned the tea shop were kind.

I was aware that those weeks of calm were largely down to Anne's presence. She might have been younger than most of the wardens, but she had principles. If she had witnessed extreme cruelty she would have spoken out.

It was on my next holiday from school that she told me she was leaving Jersey. She was emigrating to Australia. 'I'll write to you, Madeleine,' she told me. Michelle had used the same words.

I tried not to show just how much her news upset me, but it was devastating to learn that the second person I had grown to trust was leaving. Tears threatened to spill over and, seeing them, she leant over and took my hand. 'Madeleine, you're doing so well. They love you at the café and say they'll keep your job open for the next summer holiday. And there are not many summers left before you can finish school and start being completely independent. That's what I want for you. I'm going to keep in touch and you'll keep me up to date with your progress. Have we got a bargain?'

I managed a weak smile before assuring her I would. But nothing could console me for her loss. Out of all the social workers and wardens I had met, there had been only two I had trusted. One was already gone and the other was on her way.

When I left to go back to school, Morag Jordan came to the door, a complacent smirk on her face. 'I expect you'll miss Anne when you come back next time,' she said, and I read the hidden message behind her words. If I crossed her, there would be no one to rescue me from the detention cells.

CHAPTER FORTY-TWO

2011

I seem to be reliving so many events of my early life as memories suppressed for so long resurface.

When Colin Tilbrook was still at the home I was puzzled for a long time as to why so many rich, powerful men came to Haut de la Garenne. Now I believe there was a club, with its own secret codes. A club in which the unthinkable was acceptable and the members all helped each other find whatever they most desired. They were predators whose fertile hunting grounds were the institutions where society's cast-off children lived. They visited the homes under many guises, hid who they were under masks of geniality and lapped up praise for giving their time to those unfortunates.

Was Morag Jordan there when Jimmy Savile visited? I'm not sure. Not that it really matters. Colin Tilbrook almost certainly was.

I remember all of us being excited when we were told he was to visit Haut de la Garenne. We had seen him on television and could hardly believe that such a big celebrity was coming all the way to Jersey just to see us. How can I describe my first impression of him? I thought his long blond hair, big grin and oversized sunglasses made him look creepy. Sensibly I kept that to myself. It didn't take me long to recognise what he was.

I watched him chat to groups of children, chuck some under the chin, stroke a few arms as he sucked on his enormous cigar and cracked jokes. I chose not to be part of that group. Instead I stayed on the sidelines observing him.

He told the ones hanging on his every word that he wanted photographs of them all. He would sit in the middle, he added, as he expansively waved his cigar in the air.

'Wow,' was the response of all the star-struck teenagers.

They all wanted to sit next to the man who loved children, supported good causes and had politicians and royalty as his friends. The closer they were to him, the better the picture they could show around school.

'Great, sit really close,' said the reporter who, as though by magic, had turned up. 'Smile, everyone.'

The picture went into the local paper.

It made a liar of Jimmy Savile when, many years later, details of the abuse at the home surfaced and he denied making that visit.

I had mentioned his presence to the police, much to their amusement. He was still alive then, with an untarnished reputation, an OBE and a knighthood. Had he touched me, they had asked, with mocking grins and sideways glances.

'Oh, not really,' I had said. 'He just tried to grab my behind when he thought no one was looking.'

'Don't think a pat on the behind is that serious a crime, do you?' was their reply.

'I think it is,' I said indignantly, a belief they clearly did not share.

It isn't hindsight talking when I say I recognised what he was that day. There is a leer in the smile, complacency in the expression, assurance in the touching, and arrogance in the walk of the child molester: I had learnt to recognise those characteristics long before I was eleven. From when I was very young, I could tell the difference between an affectionate hug and something more sinister. I knew what old fingers groping a child's bottom meant.

'Did you tell anyone?' asked the policeman, still trying not to laugh.

'No,' was all I said then.

I wasn't going to cause them any more amusement at my expense by telling them how I had called Jimmy

Savile a dirty old man and told him to get his hands off me. His smile had slipped and, just for a second, I saw the nastiness behind the mask.

It was a year after I left the prison that the scandal of who Savile had really been shocked the world. Then the unthinkable was believed.

CHAPTER FORTY-THREE

My hope that, with the departure of Colin Tilbrook, our lives in the home would be easier lasted only a short time. When I returned after another school term, it was to find that, instead of having their brutality monitored, Morag Jordan and her husband had gained even more power.

Anthony Jordan seemed to enjoy punching and kicking children less than half his size. I can picture him now, swaggering around the corridors, his eyes glinting when he saw fear on small faces. Like him, Morag looked for the slightest reason to pick up whatever object was the nearest – a shoe, a hairbrush, a belt or even a coathanger – to hit us around the head and shoulders. But what she really took pleasure in was dragging a screaming child by their hair and locking them in a detention cell where she could reduce him or her to a cringing, terrified creature. It was she who had dreamt up stripping those she detained. Another ploy she thought of was leaving the light on in the cell so her victim couldn't even find comfort in the night's darkness. My hands would involuntarily curl into tight fists when I saw children, younger than me, being battered and terrorised. After all these years, there are still nights when the sounds of whimpering and anguished crying penetrate my sleep. With Anne gone, it appeared to me that all the remaining wardens were no better than the Jordans. There was just no concern or compassion shown to the children. If they were ill, unless it was something that required emergency hospital attention, nothing was done for them and accidental cuts and sprains were barely treated.

One incident that comes to mind still makes me cringe. He was such a little boy. Only five, he'd been transferred from the crèche and already had the haunted look of a child scared of his own shadow. Some bigger boys had taken him outside to let him play on the climbing frame. He fell. I heard his piercing scream when he landed on the lower bar. It was only when a few of us rushed out that we saw what had happened. He had landed hard on his testicles and his shrieks told us he was in terrible pain. His little face was bright red, fat tears ran down his cheeks and I realised he was stuck there.

It was one of the boys, not a warden, who lifted him off. Gently he put him on the ground and pulled down the little boy's shorts so we could see the damage. The swelling and bruising were already forming and we didn't know how to help him.

'Just leave his shorts off – the air will cool him down soon enough,' said a warden, then walked away, leaving him crying with pain.

Unable to close his legs for days, that little boy could only hobble about. Instead of the sympathy the crèche would have given him, he was mocked. 'Blue Balls', the wardens called him. 'Here comes Blue Balls.' They would collapse into laughter. I can still see his small bewildered face looking up at his tormentors.

There was no happy ending to his story, as there was not for so many of the children who were there. When he reached puberty I was no longer at the home but I heard that he was constantly bullied. The frightened child I had known became a frightened man. He had a complete breakdown when he left. Or, rather, he was diagnosed as mentally ill, once he was out of that dreadful place. The doctors were never able to rid him of his fear of the world. Now, nearly forty years later, he is still in the psychiatric hospital he was placed in as a teenager.

I think it was the same summer that that child had had his accident that builders descended on the grounds of Haut de la Garenne. A rich benefactor had decided that we would benefit from a swimming pool. There was a buzz of excitement around the home when we learnt why a large section of the grounds was being dug up.

When it was completed and filled with water, our benefactor and his wife arrived. Swimsuits were given to the girls, trunks to the boys. Speeches were made and photographs taken of happy children splashing in the water. Those were the pictures that the man took away.

We should have remembered what happened to our Christmas presents, and what we were told when we asked why they had gone. And this was the biggest present ever given to the home. The pool gave the wardens power, and Morag Jordan took full advantage of it.

'Not today,' she would say, when the sun was high in the sky and we could almost feel that cool water on our hot skin. 'You didn't make your bed properly. We have to have some discipline here.' Her list of reasons for stopping us enjoying the pool was endless. 'You were talking too loudly in the corridors' or 'I asked you to fetch coffee for us and you spilt some in the saucer.' No, 'our' pool was too good for the likes of us.

The wardens now had another recreational activity. They hosted parties to which they invited their friends, and the pool was full of tipsy adults, monopolising our present.

Then, on a particularly hot afternoon, the Jordans appeared to have a change of heart. 'You kids can go in,' they told us. It was an invitation I viewed with some suspicion and I moved as far away from them as I could. I had too many memories of the underground pool and what had been allowed to take place there ever to trust them.

'Hey,' a warden said to a pretty girl of around thirteen, 'you weren't here when the costumes were handed out,' and tossed one to her.

I watched the pretty girl, Jill, and the others who had jumped in, splashing about and wondered why the wardens had suddenly appeared so considerate. It was not until they called everyone to come and get a cold drink that I understood what they had been up to. They were all watching the pretty girl. Half smiling, she had pulled herself out and was trustingly walking towards them. Laughter rang out and the girl looked around to see what was so funny and realised they were laughing at her. She looked down at herself and her eyes widened. The water had made her swimsuit completely transparent. There was not even a towel nearby that she could cover herself with.

Jill was in the home because her mother was ill, with cancer. She had other family in Ireland. Once her mother died, and Jill understood it would happen soon, she was going to them. That she had a large family kept her safe from sexual abuse, but not from humiliation.

I guessed who had been behind that plan. It had Morag and Anthony Jordan's signature all over it.

That was the last time I saw children in the pool. I saw them near it, though: they were cleaning up after a party.

CHAPTER FORTY-FOUR

He was a boy, although his muscular body belied his age, an angry boy who enjoyed inflicting pain. I would see him in the grounds, totally absorbed in his workout regime. First the warm up, stretching, bending and running on the spot, then press-ups. From somewhere he had acquired weights, and I saw the tendons on his neck bulge as he lifted them, his vest soaked with sweat.

He took no notice of us watching him; he was far too focused on building his muscles. None of us dared tease him and even the wardens left him alone. Not that they had always done so. When his body was slight and his face smooth, he had been one of the boys taken on to the boats, the magnificent yachts owned by smiling rich men in white flannels and navy blazers. Excited little boys were promised a day out at sea, but came back changed for ever.

He was aware that I had seen him on the day he returned from his first maritime experience. He was crying, knuckles pressed hard into to his eyes to stop the tears. I had moved forwards to comfort him, for I had seen the telltale streak of blood on the back of his shorts that told me, as much as the tears did, what had taken place out there on the yacht. He brushed off my hand angrily and walked away. He never spoke to me again.

'I ain't no fucking poof,' he spat, when a man who visited the home, as many did for only one purpose, glanced in his direction.

'Faggot, fucking queer,' he snarled, towards the departing back. 'No one's going to touch me.'

I think he hoped that someone would try to lay a hand on his shoulder, whisper an unambiguous suggestion, thereby allowing that rage to escape so that he could justify his fists hammering his would-be seducer. But no one did.

He was seventeen when he raped me. I knew he was dangerous. Other girls had told me. He had attacked my friend Rachael. She cried and cried when she described how he had forced himself on her. He had pushed her to the ground, torn off her panties and brutally entered her. His grunts seemed more of anger than enjoyment.

'Why does he hate us so much?' she asked plaintively.

I didn't say: 'Because of, what was done to him.' I didn't want to offer an excuse for the person he had become because of his childhood. Instead I said I didn't know. I helped her into the bath, scooped up water and let it run down the places she couldn't reach while she scrubbed away the stink of him. Afterwards I smeared cream on to the numerous scratches and bites on her body. 'We must tell the head,' I said. 'He should be got rid of for this. He's old enough. Anyone can see what he's turned into.'

There had been rapes ever since I had been at Haut de la Garenne, but this one was different. This had not been the act of a man who enjoyed seeing fear on a child's face, or one who used status to make a frightened teenager submit. Neither was it an act of bravado in which a fellow inmate saw rape as an initiation into manhood. It had been a brutal act of hatred, not desire. He had hit Rachael so hard she had nearly blacked out. There were bruises on her face, neck and thighs. Her breasts bore the marks of his teeth and her lips were swollen because he had bitten them.

'The head would call the police if I were to take you to him,' I said.

Rachael protested. She was scared of what would happen. 'If he isn't sent away and finds out that I reported him, what might he do?' she asked. More to the point, she clearly didn't want to talk about it. She didn't expect to be shown any compassion if she did. The home closed ranks against any scandal leaking into the world outside and the police saw us as an underclass. So we kept quiet, and prayed he would leave us alone now. We hoped he might be frightened that we would make a complaint. Perhaps he would vent his anger on his workouts and concentrate on building up his body, ready for the fights he would undoubtedly get into once he left the home.

That was what I hoped, and over the next few weeks I came to believe that he was keeping his head down and marking off the days to when he could walk out through Haut de la Garenne's doors.

That hope died the day he raped me.

At sixteen I weighed just under eight stone and the self-defence moves Frank had taught me were useless against the boy in a man's body who came up behind me. His arm was round my throat before I was even aware of his presence. He was squeezing it so hard I was unable to breathe, let alone scream. His knee pushed hard into the small of my back and I went down so hard that the air whooshed out of my lungs. He turned me over and I looked into his unblinking eyes. There's no one in there, I thought, moments before his fist crashed down on the side of my head and the world began to turn black. I used every little bit of willpower to stay conscious. His chest was hovering over mine, so there was no room for me to swing my arms and thump him, though I doubt he would have felt it if I had. I could only push against something that felt like a wall of steel. I begged him to stop but it made no difference to his determination. When he entered me his hands gripped my legs so hard I felt the bruises form. He bit my breasts, covered my mouth with his, not to kiss me but to block out my screams. I had been forced to have sex many times with different men but this was worse. He wanted to hurt me. It was as though every thrust was an act of revenge for what had been done to him.

It was when the blackness returned and I felt myself losing consciousness again that he climbed off me. The sound of his footsteps walking down the cold granite corridor told me that my ordeal was over, but still I couldn't move. I wanted to, but my limbs would not obey me.

Morag Jordan found me. She didn't need to ask what had happened. Instead she helped me to my feet, put my arm around her shoulders so I could lean on her for support, then led me to her office. I heard her telling someone to fetch hot water, Dettol and antiseptic cream.

'Go and make some tea,' she told another. 'Put in plenty of sugar and she'd better have a brandy as well.' I sipped the tea, too shocked to wonder why she, of all people, was helping me. Morag swabbed the bites on my breasts with disinfectant making me gasp with pain. 'Have to do this, Madeleine,' she said firmly. 'The human bite carries more bacteria than any other and we don't want you in hospital with septicaemia, do we?'

If I had not been so dazed and in pain I might have realised that she didn't want me to end up in hospital for various reasons. Doctors are not known for covering up crimes and would be bound to report it to the police.

As she ministered to me I believed that, for the first time since I'd met her, she was being kind. This was an illusion that was quickly shattered by her next words. 'I think you and he just went too far,' I heard her say.

'He raped me,' I protested incredulously.

'Don't be silly, Madeleine. I know what you teenage girls are like. Always sniffing around the boys, especially the ones who are like grown men. Oh, you might look innocent, but just how many have you had, hey?'

I glared at through the one eye that wasn't swollen shut. 'I'm not the only one he's done it to, either.'

'Well, you're the first to complain.'

'I want to report him to the head and to the police. He's got to be stopped. He could kill someone,' I said desperately. I wanted her – everyone – to believe me. That vicious rape was just too much for me to keep quiet about.

'Well, you'd better think carefully before you do that, Madeleine,' she said.

'Let me explain something to you about what happens when a girl, especially one like you, tells the police she was raped. First, they look sceptical and act as though they don't believe her.'

'But you can see my bruises, the bite marks,' I interrupted angrily.

'They'll just say you like a bit of rough and now perhaps the boy's no longer interested in you. Happens lots of times when they get what they want. Not very nice, I know, but not against the law. The police will hint you're being vindictive because of it.'

'What happens if I tell them I want to lay charges and refuse to go away?'

'Well, it will most probably end up in court, and if you think the police can be harsh, just wait until you meet the defence barrister. He's not, I can tell you, interested in upholding the law. He just wants to win his case. Whatever he thinks deep down, he'll act as though he sees you as a cunning little slut who'll do anything to cause trouble for the boy and discredit Haut de la Garenne. He'll insinuate that you hate being a ward of court and you think this could be your escape. Not difficult when you've run away. That's something the police have on record. The defence barrister will have dug out every bit of dirt on you that he can find. Then, while you have to stand in that witness box, he'll tear you to shreds, as he shares his version of what happened with everyone there. You won't be able to hold your own against an educated, clever man such as he will be. The fact that you were not a virgin when it happened will come out. That boy's friends will stand up and say they've had you too. They'll describe in nice, colourful detail how you enticed them to have sex with you. How you twitched and moaned as you climaxed. You'll be accused of liking rough sex and the court will be told that you begged the boy to hit you. That's what will happen, Madeleine. Now is that really something you want to put yourself through? Or your mother? She'll be sitting there hearing all about her tart of a daughter.'

'But it's not true. I've never been near any of his friends. I never wanted to have sex with anyone. I was forced, you know by who.'

She stopped me then, before I could name names. 'So you say, Madeleine. Do you think anyone is going to believe that? I mean, and let's be honest here, have you ever made a formal complaint?'

'No.'

'Did you tell the nuns?'

'No.'

'Any of your social workers?'

'And what about your mother? . . . I thought not,' she said triumphantly, when I made no reply. 'Why was that?'

Because I was scared I wouldn't be believed. Because I was threatened with what would happen if I did. Because I would be blamed.

'But you know what's gone on here. You could speak up for me.'

'I don't know what you're talking about, Madeleine. I have no intention of risking my job by helping you with your complaints. So, think long and hard about what I've just told you.'

That night I fought off tears. For the first time since I had met Morag I believed she and the others who ran that home had won. My spirit was finally shattered.

I did not report the rape.

***

I cannot name the boy: to do so would make him more real, more human than my memories want to allow. He's dead now, a drug overdose. He didn't even make it to his twenty-first. He left the home and, as others before and after him, found other lost souls. Oblivion from his demons came in the form of pills and needles.

When I heard of his demise I tried not to let the picture of another boy, the small one with tears on his cheeks and blood on his shorts, stay in my mind. It was easier to remember him with his bulging muscles and hard eyes. Sometimes I wonder what might have happened if I had defied Morag Jordan and reported him. He wasn't eighteen so he would have been tried in a young offenders' court. Would he have been punished if Morag had spoken out or if he had told the court what had happened to him that sunny day on the white yacht? Would he have received help?

I had asked her the night of my rape, if she believed me.

No, she had replied. But I knew she did.

CHAPTER FORTY-FIVE

For the two days after Morag had found me, I crept around the home avoiding contact with anyone. I felt hollow, worthless. I believed that everything I had worked for was futile, and that that the dreams I had nurtured of being independent and successful had now turned to dust.

I had worked hard at my school, kept myself in clothes and a few luxuries with my summer job, and never let my optimism for the future wane. But that latest attack, that brutal rape, I could not take.

I snuck out in the grounds to smoke cigarettes, but what I really wanted was a drink. Anything to numb the pain. Alcohol, I had found, from when Colin Tilbrook had put that amber liquid into my hand, did just that.

There would be no bright future for me, I believed. There was nothing to look forward to.

My years at Haut de la Garenne flashed in front of me, the brutality and the humiliation. I had to escape it. I went to the small village of Gorey. I have no recollection of how I got there, just of being in a bar where a juke-box was playing loud music, competing with laughter and conversation. I had never felt so alone. I downed my first drink quickly, then the second and third.

'Don't you think you've had enough, dear?' asked the barman, kindly. 'Boyfriend trouble, is it? Never you mind, a pretty girl like you . . .' I didn't wait for him to tell me I would soon find another.

'Yes,' I said. 'You're right. I have had enough.'

I walked along to the pier, looked down at the sea now mirroring the blackness of the night sky. I thought of Geoffrey as I climbed on to the wall and leapt in.

Two fishermen saw me topple into the water and hauled me out. They pressed on my chest until I gasped and vomited water tinged with alcohol. A blanket covered me as, shivering with shock and cold, I was placed on a stretcher, then lifted into an ambulance. The noise of the siren barely penetrated my consciousness.

It was the following morning when the psychiatrist came. He sat beside my bed and asked why I had done it. The fishermen had told the ambulance driver that it was no accident: they had seen me throw myself in.

I had no answer except that I no longer wished to live, which wasn't the one he wanted to hear.

One of the nurses tried to get through to me. 'Did you not think, when you jumped, of all the things you would never experience again?' she asked.

Yes, I thought, willing her to be quiet. Pain and misery. That's why I did it.

Undeterred, she continued to list the things she thought might spark regret. 'The warmth of the sun on your skin, walking on the beach and feeling sand between your toes would be my first two,' I heard, before I tuned her out.

Receiving no sign of interest from me, she took the hint and walked away.

A children's officer came next and tried to elicit some response from me. I had none to give. I didn't even have the energy to pretend that, whatever the fishermen had said, it was a drunken accident so that I could leave and get it right the next time. They kept me in for another day, then transferred me to St Saviour's Psychiatric Unit.

That afternoon, a different doctor, in corduroy trousers and a tweed jacket, sat by my bed. 'You're well enough to get up, Madeleine,' he told me. 'Would you like a nurse to help you dress?'

'No,' I replied, clutching the sheet. The idea of leaving the safety of the bed made me feel as though my stomach had been invaded by a swarm of butterflies. 'I want to stay here,' I whispered.

'Why?'

'It feels safe.'

'Aren't you feeling any better?' he asked.

'No.'

He explained to me, in a voice that seemed far away, that there was a treatment he could put me on. He assured me that it would rid me of my depression. That the result was more or less instant and that the medication he could prescribe would take longer to work. The treatment he advocated was electric-shock therapy. There were a few side effects, he told me. It frequently caused loss of memory for a short time. That was the bit I latched on to: getting rid of my memories.

It appeared that the home had thought this was a good option. Their opinion had been sought.

If Morag Jordan had told them about the rape and that I was most probably suffering from post-traumatic stress disorder, my treatment might have been very different. I might have been offered psychotherapy, which is used for PTSD. And if that had happened perhaps now my memories would be clearer. But she hadn't.

CHAPTER FORTY-SIX

Once I was considered able to look after myself, the children's department found accommodation for me at Camelot, a girls' hostel. It was run by a couple who were the complete opposite to the staff at Haut de la Garenne. Warm and caring, their main aim was to ensure that the girls who lived with them were safe and happy. I stepped over their threshold into normality. They knew, of course, that I had been in the psychiatric hospital. But after my first day, when they gave me tea and cake, then told me that if I ever needed to talk their door would always be open, it was never mentioned.

Soon after I moved into Camelot, I found a job working at Summerland Knitwear Factory. I was one of the women responsible for sewing pockets onto cardigans. I silently thanked Sister Xavier, who had painstakingly taught me how to sew tiny little stitches. Because of her patience, I was praised for being neat and fast. The women I worked alongside were friendly and a couple of them were about the same age as me. To begin with I was terrified that they would find out about my time in the hospital and what I had done to be put in there. Gradually that fear faded as I realised that, as far as a girl of seventeen is concerned, people are interested in her present and future, not her past.

I was asked about boyfriends and quizzed about why I hadn't got one. They followed this with the comment that always made me cringe inside: 'A pretty girl like you' or, worse, 'A pretty little thing like you'. The shock treatment might have taken the clarity from some of my memories and muddled others, but it had not removed the feeling those words gave me.

It was a friend from work who, within a year of my arriving at Camelot, introduced me to the man who would become my husband. A new Portuguese restaurant had opened, she told me, and suggested I join her and her boyfriend for a meal. My surprise date was already in the restaurant when we arrived and my first impression of him wasn't a good one. Dark-haired and olive-skinned, he was good looking but, I thought indignantly, he certainly knew it. And, besides, as I had told my friend repeatedly, I didn't want a boyfriend. In faltering English – he had arrived In Jersey from Portugal only recently – he offered to walk me home. I refused. Would I like to go out with them after the meal for a drink? he asked. 'I don't drink,' I told him. He offered again to walk me home. I refused. When I left the restaurant I neither wanted nor expected to see him again.

A few weeks later, he found out where I lived. 'No,' I said, each time he asked me to walk with him, go for a drink, or join him and some friends for a meal. I even turned down invitations to the cinema.

It was three months before I said yes to the cinema and a meal. It was very hard for me to trust a man, but gradually I learnt to, and before I was twenty-one, I was a wife and a mother, and I was happy. Eight months later I opened the door to the police.

My mother had died. Alcohol had finally won. She had choked to death on her vomit. When I went to the chapel of rest, I thought how peaceful she looked. Death had smoothed out the lines of sadness and disappointment. I said my goodbyes to her there, rather than at the funeral, when, for Alfie's sake, I was trying to hold back my tears.

My life after that was relatively uneventful. For ten years my husband and I worked at whatever was offered. Farm work, cleaning, there was nothing I was too proud to turn a hand to. Life went by and my memories of Haut de la Garenne faded. I tried my best to be a good mother to my son. I encouraged him to do well at school: education, I told him, is important.

When I was thirty-two I had another child, a daughter. I hadn't expected to have any more but she came along and she was beautiful. Life was hard, but there were a great many wonderful elements to it. I didn't drink until 2007, the year when the police contacted me, turning my life and my family's upside down.

Over the year when I and others who had been abused were interviewed, I felt that the scabs on old wounds were being picked at for no good reason. I was convinced, as others were, that the police doubted much of what they were told. This belief was reinforced when, after only a few punishments were handed out to some of the tormentors, it appeared that the case was closed. To dredge up the memories of what had happened in Haut de la Garenne and see the scepticism on the faces of those interviewing me caused my depression to resurface. With it came the need to escape with the aid of alcohol.

Five years after the case had faded from the public eye, but not from our tortured minds, the Independent Jersey Care Inquiry reopened it. Over two hundred people gave evidence and finally had the opportunity to tell their stories without mocking smirks of disbelief.

The State of Jersey agreed that each of us who had lost their childhood deserved financial compensation. Various amounts were awarded, enough to give some of us a fresh start. Even more importantly, it gave us the dignity of finally being believed.

The adult me has learnt to count her blessings. The past, I have told myself, should never be allowed to win. It is the present and the future that are important. My two children, who I'm so proud of, have given me more support than I could ever have asked for. Even though it was not easy for me to help them with homework, for I never really mastered reading, both of them did well at school. My son, who is trilingual, went to a Spanish university, where he studied to be a priest, and my daughter has a good career in front of her. Thanks to the nuns, who taught me that everyone is special in their own way, the confidence that had been taken away from me returned.

We all still live in Jersey and, yes, memories are triggered not only by the sight of the dark grey buildings of Haut de la Garenne and St Saviour's Hospital, but by the faces of those who are lost. It is in the witching hours that my nightmares return. But in the daytime I look at the beauty of the island, see my family and friends and feel some degree of contentment.